T0328690

Cambridge Elements ☰

Elements on Women in the History of Philosophy
edited by
Jacqueline Broad
Monash University

FRANCES POWER COBBE

Alison Stone
Lancaster University

CAMBRIDGE
UNIVERSITY PRESS

CAMBRIDGE
UNIVERSITY PRESS

University Printing House, Cambridge CB2 8BS, United Kingdom

One Liberty Plaza, 20th Floor, New York, NY 10006, USA

477 Williamstown Road, Port Melbourne, VIC 3207, Australia

314–321, 3rd Floor, Plot 3, Splendor Forum, Jasola District Centre,
New Delhi – 110025, India

103 Penang Road, #05–06/07, Visioncrest Commercial, Singapore 238467

Cambridge University Press is part of the University of Cambridge.

It furthers the University's mission by disseminating knowledge in the pursuit of
education, learning, and research at the highest international levels of excellence.

www.cambridge.org
Information on this title: www.cambridge.org/9781009160971
DOI: 10.1017/9781009160964

First published 2022

A catalogue record for this publication is available from the British Library.

ISBN 978-1-009-16097-1 Paperback
ISSN 2634-4645 (online)
ISSN 2634-4637 (print)

Frances Power Cobbe

Elements on Women in the History of Philosophy

DOI: 10.1017/9781009160964
First published online: July 2022

Alison Stone
Lancaster University

Author for correspondence: Alison Stone, a.stone@lancaster.ac.uk

Abstract: This Element introduces the philosophy of Frances Power Cobbe (1822–1904), a very well-known moral theorist, advocate of animal welfare and women's rights, and critic of Darwinism and atheism in the Victorian era. After locating Cobbe's achievements within nineteenth-century British culture, this Element examines her duty-based moral theory of the 1850s and then her 1860s accounts of duties to animals, women's rights, and the mind and unconscious thought. From the 1870s, in critical response to Darwin's evolutionary ethics, Cobbe put greater moral weight on the emotions, especially sympathy. She now criticised atheism for undermining morality, emphasised women's duties to develop virtues of character, and recommended treating animals with sympathy and compassion. The Element links Cobbe's philosophical arguments to her campaigns for women's rights and against vivisection, brings in critical responses from her contemporaries, explains how she became omitted from the history of philosophy, and shows the lasting importance of her work.

This Element also has a video abstract: www.cambridge.org/alisonstone

Keywords: Frances Power Cobbe, women in the history of philosophy, nineteenth-century philosophy, history of British philosophy, animal ethics

ISBNs: 9781009160971 (PB), 9781009160964 (OC)
ISSNs: 2634-4645 (online), 2634-4637 (print)

Contents

Introduction

This Element introduces the philosophy of Frances Power Cobbe (1822–1904). Cobbe was a very well-known and highly regarded moral theorist, advocate of animal welfare and women's rights, and critic of Darwinism and atheism in the Victorian era. After placing Cobbe's life and achievements in the context of nineteenth-century British culture, this Element examines her duty-based moral theory of the 1850s. Cobbe treated religion and morality as inseparably connected, on the grounds that duty presupposes a moral law, which presupposes a divine legislator. Over the 1860s, Cobbe proceeded to set out a philosophical account of human duties to animals, a form of difference feminism, and a dualist but non-Cartesian view of mind which gave a central place to unconscious thought. From the 1870s onwards, partly in critical response to Darwin's evolutionary ethics, Cobbe's views changed. She now stressed the moral role of the emotions, particularly sympathy. She argued that Christianity cultivates sympathy and reduces our natural disposition to feel 'heteropathy', i.e., pleasure at other people's pain and pain at other people's pleasure. Cobbe now criticised atheism, agnosticism, and secularism for undermining morality and the whole of meaningful life, and she emphasised women's duties to develop and practise virtues of character across the nested circles of social life. Regarding animal welfare, she now argued that we should, above all treat animals in ways that express sentiments of sympathy and compassion for them.

This Element shows how these philosophical arguments of Cobbe's were interwoven with her practical campaigns for women's rights and against vivisection. It brings in some of the many responses to Cobbe from her interlocutors and contemporaries, including Annie Besant, Richard Holt Hutton, Charles Darwin, Henry Sidgwick, Arabella Buckley, Vernon Lee, Mrs Humphry Ward, and Anna Kingsford. The Element also puts forward an explanation for why Cobbe became left out of the history of philosophy, and demonstrates the lasting importance of her work.

1 Cobbe's Life, Writings, and Context

1.1 Cobbe's Life and Career

Frances Power Cobbe was born in 1822, the fifth child and only daughter of Charles Cobbe and Frances Conway. The Cobbes were a landed family who lived at Newbridge near Dublin. They were part of the ruling Protestant elite in Ireland during the period when the country was incorporated into the United Kingdom. But although Cobbe was part of the ruling elite, she had to watch her older brothers go to boarding school, destined for university and the professions, while she remained at home, educated by governesses with a view to making her an 'Ornament of Society', as she put it (Cobbe 1894: vol. 1: 56). She disparaged her education, particularly its closing chapter at a finishing school in Brighton. Since the curriculum covered English, French, German, Italian, music, dancing, and Bible study, it was not as desultory as Cobbe made out. Certainly it left her a voracious reader and writer. On returning to the family home in Ireland, Cobbe took the continuation of her studies into her own hands. Supplementing her family's extensive holdings in religion and theology with subscriptions to several libraries, she taught herself history, classical and modern literature, ancient philosophy, architecture, astronomy, and – with lessons from a local parson – Greek and geometry. She also read as much non-Western religion and philosophy as was then available in translation.

Charles Cobbe was an evangelical Christian who emphasised sin and eternal punishment and maintained a strict religious atmosphere. Cobbe was uncomfortable with this, and her religious doubts escalated over her teenage years. By the age of twenty, she was suffering from a crisis of faith. But she refused to give up on God or write Him off as unknowable. She investigated deism, natural theology, German biblical criticism, Unitarianism, and the humane and optimistic theology of the American Transcendentalist Theodore Parker. Parker's work was decisive for her; she went on to correspond with him and edit his collected works. Parker's views inspired her 'system of Theism' (Cobbe 1864: 157) which, contrary to Charles Cobbe, stressed love and forgiveness, universal salvation, and the compatibility of reason and conscience.

This period of intensive religious study and reflection on Cobbe's part coincided with the Irish potato famine, which began in 1845 and was a formative experience for her (see O'Connor 2017). The famine reinforced ʹ her determination to find a meaning and religious framework for making sense of suffering, as well as her sense that she must be useful to others. It was another great blow when her adored mother died in 1847 but, again, Cobbe responded with a determination to devise a philosophical and religious system that made room for personal immortality and, therefore, for the possibility and hope of reunion with loved ones after we die. Her developing views enraged her father. He expelled her from the family home, although she used the ensuing period at her brother's farm in Donegal productively, writing a long 'Essay on True Religion' in 1849. Shortly afterwards, her father recalled her to manage the house at Newbridge. Cobbe still found time amidst her many household duties to rewrite the 'Essay on True Religion' as her first book, the *Essay on Intuitive Morals* of 1855–7.

Just after *Intuitive Morals* Volume Two came out, Charles Cobbe died. Cobbe used her new-found freedom to travel, unaccompanied, around Europe and the

Near East. But she continued to feel that she must be useful and took a position in Bristol helping the pioneering educational reformer Mary Carpenter, who ran a ragged school for poor and destitute girls. Carpenter's rather spartan lifestyle did not suit Cobbe, though; devout as Cobbe was, she was never one for stinting on life's pleasures. She left Carpenter's establishment and focussed on writing. Initially, she drew on her experiences with Carpenter to address welfare reform, effectively advocating an early form of the welfare state. Then Cobbe followed up in the early 1860s with a string of powerful journal articles on women's and animal rights and the book *Broken Lights* on theology and philosophy of religion. These acclaimed writings propelled her rapidly to the centre of intellectual life in Britain. By the mid-1860s, she could support herself financially by writing, and she settled in London with the sculptor Mary Lloyd, with whom she would live for the next thirty years. Cobbe and Lloyd were tacitly acknowledged as a couple, being invited together to dinner parties and social events, and hosting many of their own. Everyone sought Cobbe's company, and she got to know countless leading intellectual lights – Josephine Butler, Darwin, Thomas Henry Huxley, John Stuart Mill, Mary Somerville, and Herbert Spencer, to mention just a few.

Cobbe became drawn into the gathering wave of agitation for women's rights. For example, she was one of the women who collected signatures for a petition for women's suffrage which Mill presented to parliament – to no avail – in 1866. But suffrage by no means exhausted Cobbe's concerns or those of other first-wave feminists. Cobbe campaigned for women's education and rights to hold professional jobs, and for married women's property rights and protection against domestic violence – in a context where women had none of these things. Incidentally, it is to Cobbe that we owe the image of the 'first wave'; she wrote:

> An immense wave is lifting up women all over the world; and, if we 'survey womankind from China to Peru', we shall find in almost every country of the globe . . . a new demand for education, for domestic freedom, and for civil and political rights, made by women on behalf of their sex. (Cobbe 1881a: 22)

But there was another political issue that was even dearer to Cobbe's heart: anti-vivisection. She led the British campaign first to regulate the practice and then, finding the regulatory legislation that was passed in 1876 unacceptably weak, to abolish vivisection outright. She founded two anti-vivisection organisations – first the Victoria Street Society in 1875 and then, when she thought it had become too conciliatory with the status quo, the British Union for the Abolition of Vivisection in 1898. Both still exist as the National Anti-Vivisection Society and Cruelty Free International. It was Cobbe, more than anyone else, who put the moral status of animals and the legitimacy of animal experimentation on the social and political agenda.

Throughout this whirl of activity, Cobbe remained remarkably prolific. She published dozens of articles in most of the leading heavyweight journals of the time as well as several books. Especially given the highly patriarchal context, what she achieved is astonishing. She continued writing well into the 1890s, by which time she and Lloyd had moved to Lloyd's native Wales – Lloyd had never been happy in the metropolis. After Lloyd died in 1896 Cobbe remained in Wales for her last years – she died in 1904 – while continuing to try to steer the now immense, and increasingly faction-riven, anti-vivisection struggle.[1]

Throughout Cobbe's life, her writing was always in demand and many of her journal essays were gathered into books: *Essays on the Pursuits of Women* (Cobbe 1863); *Studies New and Old of Ethical and Social Subjects* (Cobbe 1865); *Darwinism in Morals, and Other Essays* (Cobbe 1872a); *The Hopes of the Human Race, Hereafter and Here* (Cobbe 1874b); *The Peak in Darien, with some other Inquiries Touching Concerns of the Soul and the Body* (Cobbe 1882b); *The Scientific Spirit of the Age* (Cobbe 1888c); and *The Modern Rack: Papers on Vivisection* (Cobbe 1889). She published an autobiography (Cobbe 1894), a second book on theology called *Dawning Lights* (Cobbe 1868a), the lecture series *The Duties of Women* (Cobbe 1881a), travel writing, and a large volume of news reporting. As this indicates, not all her writing was philosophical: for instance, from 1868 to 1875 she wrote the leaders for the high-circulation newspaper *The Echo*. She still wove some philosophy into her columns, as when wondering whether a conjoined twin would ever experience themselves as an 'I' or whether the other twin could ever 'form for [them], as the Germans say, a part of the *"Nicht-Ich"*, the "Not-I"' (Cobbe 1876: 245). Even when Cobbe addressed topical and current affairs, then, she tended to bring a philosophical underpinning.

Her philosophical standpoint evolved over time, as I will trace in this Element. A major change occurred in the 1870s. In the 1850s and 1860s, Cobbe sought to reconcile reason and faith, science and conscience; she intended to 'harmonise the Intellect and the Religious Sentiment' (Cobbe 1864: 157). Over the 1870s she ceased to believe that harmonisation was possible. This change of mind was bound up with her political involvement on two fronts – one successful, for legislation to protect women from domestic violence; the other less successful, for the restriction then abolition of

---

[1] For more detail on Cobbe's life, see the biographies by Mitchell (2004) and Williamson (2005). Two other excellent books on Cobbe are Peacock (2002), on her ethical and religious thought, and Hamilton (2006), on her feminism and her career in writing for the periodical press. An indicative guide to further reading on Cobbe is Stone (2022b).

vivisection. Her research into 'wife-torture' and 'animal-torture' brought her face to face with some horrendous and gratuitous cruelty and made her much more pessimistic about human beings, convinced that our evolutionary heritage has left us with savage and cruel passions. She stressed the need for the joint forces of religion and law to educate and soften our emotions and instil in us love, sympathy, and compassion for the weak and those in need – a spirit of selfless love that she related to the Christian idea of agape.

Cobbe now saw atheism as fatally weakening religion's educative powers, and science, especially evolutionary theory, as championing the 'survival of the fittest' (in Herbert Spencer's phrase) and the rights of the strong over the weak. To Cobbe, evolutionism was the theory and vivisection was the practice. She satirised the 'morals of evolution' thus:

> Nature is extremely cruel, but we cannot do better than follow Nature; and the law of the 'Survival of the Fittest', applied to human agency, implies the absolute right of the Strong (i.e., those who can prove themselves 'Fittest') to sacrifice the Weak and Unfit. (Cobbe 1889: 66)

She said this, we should recall, at a time when eugenics was on the rise. In contrast, Cobbe was adamant that we have duties to care for the weak, the infirm, and the needy even if this goes against nature and laws of natural selection. We can do better than follow nature; we can follow the moral law instead. On that key point she never wavered.

1.2 Print Culture in Nineteenth-Century Britain

To understand the character of Cobbe's philosophical writing, we need to contextualise it in the print culture of nineteenth-century Britain – the scale of which was vast. 'The sheer volume and diversity of printed matter was unprecedented' (Taunton 2014). In terms of books, by 1900 about 7,000 new titles were being published each year. But even more important than books were periodicals, which reached larger audiences because they were cheaper. At least 125,000 journals, magazines, and newspapers came and went over the nineteenth century. Of these, the heavyweight periodicals were central in shaping informed public opinion. Early in the century, these periodicals were headed by the triad of the liberal *Edinburgh Review*, the conservative *Quarterly Review*, and the radical *Westminster Review*. In mid-century, these were displaced by *Fraser's*, *Macmillan's*, and *Cornhill Magazines*, and later in the century *The Nineteenth Century* and *Contemporary Review* came to the fore. Cobbe published very regularly in *Fraser's*, *Macmillan's*, the *Contemporary*, and many other journals, besides founding two journals herself to disseminate anti-vivisection ideas, *The Zoophilist* (1881–96) and *The Abolitionist* (1899–1949).

Nineteenth-century periodical culture in Britain was very different from that of modern specialist academic journals. First, it was *generalist*. Writers from what we now regard as different disciplines all intervened on issues together (e.g., on the mind and its relations to the brain), debating one another in a common language. These authors tackled issues in a non-technical, wide-ranging, and opinionated way, and they treated religious concerns as integral to every topic, for Victorian culture was highly devout.[2] The wide-ranging and generalist character of these debates meant that philosophical questions about basic principles and assumptions were never far away. Second, the journals operated on the model of '*debate in serial form*' (Hamilton 2012: 37; my emphasis). For example, Cobbe wrote the ironically titled 'What Shall We Do with Our Old Maids?' in response to William Rathbone Greg's 'Why Are Women Redundant?', and she wrote 'Agnostic Morality' in response to Vernon Lee's 'Responsibilities of Unbelief', to which Lee replied in turn with 'The Consolations of Belief'. Third, these journal debates shaded seamlessly into *wider public debates*. This was because journals shaded into magazines and magazines into newspapers, while journals were widely read in the first place because they were non-specialist.

These features of periodical culture meant that Cobbe could use her preferred medium, the journal essay, to do philosophy in a public setting. Her philosophising was thus generalist. She was not a professional specialist but did philosophy – like her contemporaries, Mill for instance – in a way that continually overlapped with questions of religion, culture, politics, and society. After all, philosophy as a specialist profession had not yet formed. The academic disciplines as we know them today, with their specialist organs and institutions, only began to be established in Britain from the 1870s onwards. This is important for it meant that, although women could not hold academic posts or even go to university for much of the century, this did not automatically cut women out of philosophical discussion, since the latter went on in a generalist setting anyway.

But, one might ask, how could women participate in debates in the periodicals, given patriarchal assumptions about women not being up to the life of the mind? Here another key feature of periodical culture came into play: anonymity. Early in the century, the convention was for all journal articles to be anonymous. The principle for articles to be signed only came in gradually over the century, and in the teeth of considerable resistance. The editors of the first volume of *The Wellesley Index to Victorian Periodicals* estimate that, up until 1870, around

---

[2] As the century went on, ever more varieties of belief and unbelief proliferated (see Hetherington and Stainthorp 2020). But these often inherited the spiritual intensity and zeal of older religious outlooks – secularism and alternative religions thus remained indebted to Christianity even while criticising it.

97 per cent of articles were anonymous (see *Wellesley Index* 2006–21). Anonymity enabled women to publish without being censured for doing so. Once signatures began to come in, women continued to protect themselves as best they could; they sometimes remained anonymous anyway, or used initials (e.g., 'A. B.' for Arabella Buckley), or pseudonyms (e.g., 'George Eliot', 'Vernon Lee'), or first initials in place of given names (e.g., 'H. P. Blavatsky', 'V. Welby').[3]

Crucial as anonymity was in allowing women to take part in intellectual life, Cobbe herself was an outlier since, apart from her first book *Intuitive Morals*, virtually everything she published was signed with her full female name. This tells us, first, about 'the position Miss Cobbe [held] in Intellect and Thought' (as her defender Charles Adams put it to her critic Richard Owen; see Mitchell 2004: 284). Cobbe had a level of authority usually reserved for men. She was almost always listed – alongside Mary Somerville, Harriet Martineau, and George Eliot – as one of the great intellectual women of the age. Take, for instance, Annie Besant's objection to opponents of women's rights:

> If this natural mental inferiority of women be a fact, ... [then] Mary Somerville, Mrs Lewis [*sic*] (better known as George Eliot), Frances Power Cobbe, Harriet Martineau, were made, I suppose, when nature was asleep.
>
> (Besant 1885b: 333)

Second, Cobbe's use of her signature, exceptional in this period, tells us that – despite the male reviewers who repeatedly praised her 'masculine penetration of mind' (Réville 1875: 56) – she was proud to write as a woman. One of her favourite expressions was 'I am a *woman*. Nothing concerning the interests of women is alien to me', adapting the famous adage of Terence 'I am a man – nothing human is alien to me' (Mitchell 2004: 333). When Cobbe's critics put to her that she only defended animals because she was a sentimental woman, she answered:

> I do not in the smallest degree object to finding my appeals ... treated as womanly. I claim, as a woman ... the better right to be heard in such a cause than a man. ... If my sex has a 'mission' of any kind, it is surely to soften this hard world. (Cobbe 1895: 497)

Let us explore how Cobbe tried to do so.

2 Moral Theory

2.1 *Intuitive Morals*

Cobbe's first book was the *Essay on Intuitive Morals*. It 'served me, personally', she said, 'as a scaffolding for all my life-work, a key to open most of the locks

---

[3] On the positives of anonymity for women, see Easley (2004).

which might have barred my way' (Cobbe 1894: vol. 1: 98). Initially, it came out anonymously. Volume One, *Theory of Morals*, appeared in 1855 and Volume Two, *Religious Duty*, in 1857. Both volumes were reissued in 1864 under Cobbe's name, because she had become well known in the meantime. In this section, I focus on Volume One, which sets out Cobbe's duty-based moral theory.

Not short of ambition, Cobbe proposed a new 'System of Morals better than any of those which are current among us', a system that treated the 'Law of Right' as an end in itself that transcends the empirical, natural world (Cobbe 1855: v, vi). However, Cobbe also said that she was merely popularising existing moral theories such as Kant's (vi). But this should not mislead us,[4] for she immediately clarified that she was no 'exact exponent' of Kant or anyone else. Rather, she intended to 'unite into one homogeneous and self-consistent whole the purest and most enlarged theories ... on ethical science' (vi). Her simultaneous assertion and denial of her originality reflects the fact that it was then widely thought that women could not produce original ideas but only reproduce the ideas of men, whether by popularising, translating, commentating, or educating the public. To avoid criticism, therefore, women often described their work as 'merely popularising' even when they were advancing original views, and Cobbe's vacillation typifies this.[5]

The scope of *Theory of Morals* is broad. Cobbe argues that duties presuppose a moral law, which presupposes a divine legislator. She then explains why God has created us as morally imperfect beings, why duty has priority over virtue and happiness, that there must be an afterlife in which we can continue to make moral progress, and why utilitarianism and other happiness-based moral theories are deficient. The book also includes an intuitionist account of moral knowledge and a voluntarist theory of moral agency.

Here, I will concentrate on three strands of Cobbe's theory: (1) the indissoluble link she makes between religion and morality, (2) why and how she puts duty

---

[4] Unfortunately, it often has misled people, even scholars of Cobbe's work such as Williamson, who states: '*Intuitive Morals* was not an original work' (Williamson 2005: 29). Cobbe's champion Frank Newman (the brother of the better-known Cardinal Newman) criticised Cobbe for giving this misleading impression: 'she commits the great unfairness to her own moral system ... of insisting that it shall be received through the doors of the Kantian philosophy' (Newman 1865: 271).

[5] For example, in the obituary that Harriet Martineau wrote for herself when she (mistakenly) expected to die soon, she foreswore any originality: 'she could popularize, while she could neither discover nor invent' (Martineau 1877: vol. 2: 572–3). As Deirdre David puts it, Martineau intended to 'perform ... work of auxiliary usefulness in the service of theories she never claims to have originated' (David 1987: 71). As with Cobbe, Martineau's self-descriptions should not be taken at face value; but they are telling about the climate of the time.

before happiness, and (3) the nature of her intuitionism. These strands are crucial for both *Intuitive Morals* and the subsequent development of Cobbe's thought.

2.2 Morality and Religion

Cobbe's theory starts from the concept of duty. A duty is something one is obliged to do or refrain from doing (Cobbe 1855: 8). Such obligations hold for all rational agents, i.e., all beings that can both grasp what is obligatory and do it because it is obligatory. Collectively, duties make up the moral law (9), and a law presupposes a legislator. It cannot be us who legislate the moral law to ourselves, as Kant thought. For 'it is needful to guard against the errors of applying to this underived law the analogies of human derived legislation. . . . It is not the standard of Right, which is, or can be, shifted so as to conduce to our beatification' (10–11). Cobbe's point is that the moral law binds us absolutely and exists prior to our wills – it is 'underived'. What the law specifies to be right is always and forever right and cannot change: 'The moral character of good and evil is a real, universal, and eternal distinction, existing through all worlds and for ever' (11). This can only be possible if the law is prescribed by an authority higher, and more constant and ultimate, than volatile human agents. The law must therefore come from God.

For Cobbe, then, the moral law is a religious law through and through, so that in doing what is right, we obey God's will. 'Morality necessarily includes Religion, and . . . the same Intuition which teaches us disinterested obedience to the Law because it is Right, teaches us also disinterested Obedience to that Will which is Righteous' (193). There can be no atheist morality, because there is 'no true virtue without Piety' (203).

Cobbe regards religion and morality as inextricable for a further reason too: morality requires an afterlife, and this presupposes a religious framework. Cobbe elaborates as follows. Because God exists, He must have created us, and created us as moral agents capable of following the law. Yet, manifestly, we are all morally imperfect. We often fail to do what is right, and we see others around us failing too. We can only reconcile our being made for virtue with our imperfection if we assume that we have immortal souls that go on progressing morally in the afterlife (39–43). Without this, our moral efforts will come to seem pointless, and the moral law will cease to motivate us. We must be immortal for morality to be possible.

2.3 Duty before Happiness

For Cobbe, we must do what the moral law obliges us to do, irrespective of our desires; the law is an end in itself. She thus opposed happiness-based moral theories. Defining happiness as 'the gratification of all the desires of our compound nature, … moral, intellectual, affectional, and sensual' (142), she classified and rejected several happiness-based theories, including *euthumism* and *private and public eudaimonism*.

2.3.1 Euthumism

What Cobbe calls 'euthumism' – and what we today would call 'virtue ethics' – is the view that we should obey the moral law for the sake of having a virtuous character. This is taken to be desirable because it gives us moral pleasure: 'the pursuit of virtue for the sake of its intrinsic, *i.e.* Moral pleasure, [is] … euthumism' (142). Thus, of the several components of the compound *happiness*, euthumists foreground moral happiness. Their view is that 'the Moral Pleasure, the peace and cheerfulness of mind, and applause of Conscience enjoyed in virtue [are] the proper motive for its practice' (143). Cobbe associates euthumism with the ancients: Democritus, Cicero, the Epicureans, and Stoics (144).

She objects that euthumism gives the wrong reason for obeying the moral law: first, because for euthumists the agent's 'desire is for his *own* Moral pleasure' (143), and he is not concerned for others for their own sake; second, because this slides into spiritual pride, performing actions to obtain a pleasant sense of self-approbation (147–8); and third, because euthumism cannot accommodate cases where we must do something – punishing a criminal, reproving a child, renouncing an unworthy friend – even though it is wholly painful (148).

2.3.2 Private Eudaimonism

What Cobbe calls 'private eudaimonism' is a form of utilitarianism on which each individual can only pursue their own individual happiness, or ought to pursue only this because they have no reason or motivation to do anything else. Cobbe rejects this as no 'System of Morals' at all (69), because it is entirely selfish, entailing, for example, that A can only ever perform an act of charity to B to obtain the benefit of B's gratitude (148). Private eudaimonists try to get around this selfishness problem by including moral pleasure along with the other components of happiness which motivate us to action. But: 'Eudaimonists confound *Affectional* with *Moral* Pleasures when they imagine they enjoy the latter for an action done from motives of interest' (148). That is, the theory trades on a conflation of moral and affective pleasure, when really these are distinct and the theory only has room for the latter. Thus, it remains a creed of selfishness.

2.3.3 Public Eudaimonism

'Public eudaimonism' is the more familiar form of utilitarianism on which we should act to produce the greatest happiness of the greatest number (149). But Cobbe says, for utilitarians, the reason why this is what we must do is that every individual in fact wants their own happiness. Since everyone wants their own happiness, though, this is in fact what they invariably pursue or is all that they have reason to pursue (as on private eudaimonism). Therefore, individuals either cannot pursue the general happiness or have no rational grounds to do so unless it directly coincides with their individual happiness. Yet, the two often conflict. In such cases of conflict, 'What motive remains to induce us to sacrifice the very smallest of our pleasures …?' (70). The public eudaimonist might reply that increasing the general happiness gives us moral pleasure, but for Cobbe, this again illicitly conflates moral and affectional pleasure. The upshot is that the public eudaimonist really gives us no basis for obeying the duty to increase the general happiness.

Cobbe reiterated this core criticism of utilitarianism tirelessly across all her work: *either* utilitarianism wrongly vindicates personal selfishness, *or* it prescribes a duty to increase the general welfare for which it cannot account and which only makes sense within a non-utilitarian, duty-based framework.

2.4 Intuitionism

Cobbe maintains that basic moral principles are known through a priori intuition, along with basic mathematical and geometrical principles. Ethics is therefore an exact science like pure mathematics or geometry, rather than an experimental science in which a priori and sensory knowledge work together (45–50). But what are 'a priori intuitions'? For Cobbe, moral principles are known intuitively in several senses:

i. They are known immediately, prior to any sensory input (67–70). The central contrast is with the view that we obtain our knowledge of moral principles inductively. Cobbe, like many nineteenth-century moral theorists, saw utilitarianism as an inductive moral theory (69–70): the utilitarian starts by observing the world around us, reaches the generalisation that all individuals always desire their own happiness, and further generalises to the law that we ought to increase the general happiness. For Cobbe, it is this inductive starting-point that leads utilitarianism ineluctably into selfishness, because 'the adherent of … Eudaimonism is logically bound to confine his reasoning to those consequences of [affectional] pleasure and pain which are visibly attached in this life to good and evil actions' (69).

ii. Moral principles are known deductively, independently of sensory evidence, starting from the concept of duty and deriving rationally what it implies (68).

iii. The moral law really exists independently of our minds (6–7), laid down by God. We 'intuit' this law in apprehending that it is there anyway, whatever we may happen to think about moral matters (7).

iv. The moral law is revealed in our conscience, the faculty that God has given us for apprehending His law: 'intuition' is 'God's tuition' (37), and '*the voice of God must speak truth*' (67).

We may well wonder whether these several senses of intuition are compatible with one another. Cobbe thought they were. She was not alone in treating morality as intuitive along these lines. Intuitionism and utilitarianism were the two dominant alternative moral theories in nineteenth-century Britain. Consequently, Cobbe's intuitionism faced challenges from those who leaned to the utilitarian side. One of these challengers was Cobbe's former devotee turned militant secularist, Annie Besant.

2.5 Besant's Criticisms

Initially an evangelical Christian, Besant underwent a crisis of faith in the early 1870s. She held onto her faith for a while by adopting Cobbe's theism (Besant 1893: 106–7). But Besant's religious doubts quickly resurfaced and, in late 1874, she renounced Christianity and became an atheist (Besant 1893: 145). She joined the National Secular Society and became one of its leaders, championing secularism, utilitarianism, and – in the 1880s – Fabian socialism, before turning her back on all this in 1889 and converting to the alternative religion Theosophy.

Having become a secularist, Besant sharply criticised Cobbe's intuitionism in several writings, including 'The True Basis of Morality', an 1874 talk that was repeatedly reissued as a free-standing pamphlet (Besant 1882a) and was directed against 'Miss Frances Power Cobbe, one of the best-known leaders of the Theistic and intuitional school' (Besant 1882a: 10). Besant argued as follows:

i. Intuition is a subjective faculty and cannot yield knowledge of objective moral laws, which can be gained only by observing nature. Just as with physical laws, to know anything objective, we must begin with observation.

ii. Intuition would only be reliable if there were universal agreement about what intuition reveals. But, actually, what counts as intuitive varies in different societies, times, and places. So, 'is there any particular reason why *our* intuition should be *the* intuition?' (Besant 1882a: 7). How do we decide between competing intuitions?

iii. In fact, Besant says, we *can* trust modern, civilised, European 'intuitions', but only because they are 'the result of transmitted moral tendencies ... [that] arise from our ancestors having done [certain] actions for generation after generation' (Besant 1882a: 8). Contrary to Cobbe, these 'intuitions' are not a direct line to God but are merely our inherited moral responses, embodying accumulated human wisdom. This does not reduce them to unwarranted prejudices. They offer us fair starting hypotheses about what is right, from which we can gather observations and place morality onto a scientific basis.

iv. Based on informed and impartial observation, we rise to grasp the general law that every individual desires happiness and, from there, that the right thing to do is always whatever increases the general happiness. Repeated observation tells us which classes of action practically serve this goal. Scientifically based morality is utilitarian.

v. Cobbe's objections to utilitarianism do not stick. In particular, Besant rejects Cobbe's arguments against private and public eudaimonism:

> Opponents of utilitarianism generally fall into the error of speaking of the happiness which is set forward as the criterion of morality, as though it only included the lower kinds of pleasure and animal enjoyment. But the happiness which is intended by utilitarians includes every possible phase of physical, mental, and moral enjoyment. Miss Cobbe ought not to fall into this common misrepresentation, for she begins by rightly defining happiness as the gratification of all the desires of our nature: she then somewhat oddly argues that happiness cannot be the true end of life, because we must often resign some of the desires of our nature in order to do right. If utilitarians aimed at securing perfect happiness, which is impossible, her arguments would have some force, but as they only aim at securing the greatest attainable amount of happiness, this portion of her strictures falls to the ground. (Besant 1882a: 10)

In other words, because Cobbe has admitted that moral happiness is one component of happiness, she ought to allow that we can be motivated to pursue the (multi-form) happiness of others, because this fosters our own moral happiness. This motivation remains even if we have to sacrifice some of our physical and affective happiness along the way, because moral happiness is the highest, most satisfying form of happiness. True fulfilment comes from doing one's duty to others, and the utilitarian can accommodate this (11–12).

Besant's and Cobbe's disagreement concerned the basis and motivation of morality more than its substantial content. But what substantial moral obligations did Cobbe think we have? Initially, she planned to enumerate our duties in the second volume of *Intuitive Morals*. But, in the end, the latter only dealt with religious duty, i.e., duties to God. Our duties to ourselves and others instead became the focus of Cobbe's subsequent work, to which we now turn.

3 Rights of Women

3.1 Cobbe's Activism and Analysis

Cobbe campaigned and argued for women's rights against the background of a highly patriarchal society. For most of the century, women could not go to university, and often they received only limited formal education.[6] On marriage, women were legally incorporated under their husbands, against whom they retained no rights. Women could not hold professional positions; married women's property legally belonged to their husbands; and, since women could neither vote nor hold political office, it was difficult for them to engineer change to any of these arrangements.

Cobbe argued that women should have complete civil and political equality with men. She advocated female suffrage on numerous occasions (e.g., Cobbe 1869a, 1874a). She urged that women should be allowed into higher education, to graduate with university degrees, and to follow the same syllabi and be held to the same academic standards as men (Cobbe 1863: 216–39). She argued that women needed legal protection from domestic violence in a merciless critique of 'wife-torture' (Cobbe 1878), which influenced the passage of the Matrimonial Causes Act that same year. This law gave women of violent husbands the right to obtain a legal separation, retain custody of their children, and receive maintenance from the estranged husbands.

Underpinning Cobbe's recommendations for change was her theoretical account of the sources of women's subjection. The unequal structure of the family was, she concurred with Mill, 'the citadel of the enemy', i.e., it was the centre of male dominance (Mill 1869: 152). But, she added, '[W]e need to go even deeper than Mr. Mill to get at the root of the matter' (Cobbe 1869b: 366). Behind unequal family structure lay an inequality in *relations between selves,* in which 'the woman is absorbed in the man, and the man in – himself'. The male self was inflated to the centre of the universe, with women considered only in terms of their significance for men (Cobbe 1869c: 6–7, 21–23). The family in practice enshrined 'Selfism' for men and selflessness for women (Cobbe 1863: 40) because of this underlying asymmetrical structure of personal relations.

---

[6] Bedford College for women was founded in London in 1849 but only acquired degree-conferring powers in 1900. The University of London began to admit women in 1868 but did not allow them to graduate until 1878. Girton College Cambridge and Somerville College Oxford were founded respectively in 1869 and 1879. Women were not allowed to graduate, though, until 1920 at Oxford and 1948 at Cambridge.

In her 1860s essays on women, Cobbe criticised the male-centred family and argued that the ideal of women as 'the angel in the house' defeated itself. Women were expected to devote themselves to being loving wives. But there could be no genuine love between men and women if the two were so unequal that their minds could never meet, if women were so degraded that their husbands could not respect them, and if women were so dependent economically that they would inevitably marry for subsistence, not love. Under the present conditions, a woman entering marriage was like being eaten by a tarantula:

> [F]or the most absolute type of Union of all, we must seek an example in the Tarantula Spider ... when one of these delightful creatures is placed ... with a companion of his own species ... [he] gobbles him up; making him ... 'bone of his bone' (supposing tarantulas to have any bones) 'and flesh of his flesh'. The operation being completed, the victorious spider visibly acquires double bulk, and thenceforth may be understood to 'represent the family' in the most perfect manner conceivable. (Cobbe 1868b: 789)

For the time being, Cobbe suggested, women might be best off being celibate or living with other women (as she did with Mary Lloyd). But, ultimately, for loving marriages between men and women to become possible, women must retain legal personality and property on marriage and be allowed to enter jobs and professions and lead independent lives: 'To be truly the "Angel in the House," she must have kept, and ofttimes used, the wings which should lift her *above* the house, and all things in it' (Cobbe 1869c: 14). Cobbe thus tried to appeal to the patriarchs on their own ground: for marriage to realise ideals of love and community and not resemble an overgrown carnivorous spider, it had to become equal.

3.2 'What Shall We Do with Our Old Maids?'

One of the most far-reaching of Cobbe's earlier essays on women was 'What Shall We Do with Our Old Maids?', published in *Fraser's Magazine* in 1862. It was a reply to 'Why Are Women Redundant?' by the maverick political thinker William Rathbone Greg, also from 1862. Greg, in turn, was responding to the findings of the British 1861 census that women outnumbered men by half a million and that the country contained 2.5 million unmarried women who could not support themselves. His proposed solution was that these 'surplus women' should mass-migrate overseas.

Cobbe replied that these so-called 'surplus women' need not be an economic drain on society but could positively benefit everyone, themselves included, if they could only obtain an education, hold jobs, and participate in all social activities. Mass emigration was an unnecessary counsel of despair. To show the benefits that could be expected from women's participation, Cobbe classified human activities in terms of the three great guiding values of Truth, Goodness, and Beauty, corresponding respectively to the pursuit of knowledge, philanthropy, and art (Cobbe 1862: 600). Bracketing philanthropy (which she addressed elsewhere), she expanded on knowledge and, especially, art.

3.2.1 Women's Views of Truth

We need women, Cobbe says,

> to give us those views of truth which are naturally the property of woman. . . . [Just as] we need two eyes to see the roundness and fulness of objects, so in philosophy we need to behold every great truth from two standpoints . . . [T]o reach these completed views we need each side by turns to be presented to us . . . by the alternate action of men's and women's minds on each other. (610)

We cannot possibly know the whole truth on any matter unless we have men's *and* women's epistemic contributions – an early anticipation of feminist standpoint epistemology.

3.2.2 Female Artistic Genius

Regarding art, Cobbe observed that until recently critics doubted 'the possibility of women possessing any creative artistic power' (602). Women had been duped into underrating their own abilities and limited themselves to making weak, ethereal 'sweet verses and soft pictures'. No longer. With the poetry of Elizabeth Barrett Browning, the painting of Rosa Bonheur, and the sculpture of Harriet Hosmer women have embraced strength and power.

> *Now,* women who possess any real genius, apply it to the creation of what they (and not society for them) really admire. A woman naturally admires power, force, grandeur. It is these qualities, then, which we shall see more and more appearing as the spontaneous genius of woman asserts itself. (605)

Interestingly, here Cobbe identifies sculpture as the supreme art. It was common in the nineteenth century for aestheticians to classify and hierarchically rank the arts, and Cobbe devised her own hierarchical taxonomy of the arts (Cobbe 1865: 289–358), as well as addressing art and morality (Cobbe 1865: 261–88). Sculpture was usually ranked low in these scales of arts because it was material and corporeal. Cobbe in 'Old Maids', though, holds that the true work of sculpting consists in the initial design and the realising of that design in a small-scale model. As such, sculpture, of all the arts, most closely recapitulates God's act of creating the world. This is why 'Sculpture is the noblest of the arts' (Cobbe 1862: 604). Moreover, any heavy work of wrestling with large masses of clay, stone, or marble is mere implementation that assistants can carry out under the artist's direction. Because the core of sculpture is actually the initial design, women are quite capable of excelling, Cobbe's case in point being 'Harriet Hosmer, whose Zenobia ... is a definite proof that a woman can make a statue of the very highest order. ... Here is what we wanted. A woman ... can be a sculptor, and a great one' (604–5).

3.2.3 Cobbe's Difference Feminism

Cobbe's view was that women should be allowed to do all the same activities as men. For example, she thought that women did not need special educational curricula – as many people advocated at the time – but should study the very same things as men. There need be no fear that this would turn women into surrogate men and take away women's femininity, because women are necessarily different from men. Given the same subject-matters to study as men, women will still approach them *as* women, because: 'It is not in the *truths to be acquired*, but in the *assimilation of those truths* in the mind which receives them, that the difference consists' (Cobbe 1863: 226). Allowed to practise the arts, women will make art as women and realise distinctly female forms of genius; allowed to philosophise, women will look at the truth with female eyes; and so on. For Cobbe, women and men can safely be treated entirely alike in their civil and political rights and opportunities because women and men are essentially different anyway.

> Our affair is to give nature its fullest, healthiest play and richest culture, and then the result will be ... a true woman: a being, not artificially different from a man, but radically and essentially, because *naturally* different. (Cobbe 1863: 226–7)

Women's expression of their distinct nature in art, philosophy, philanthropy, etc., is valuable for women themselves, and for everyone else, since we need two pairs of eyes to see things in the round. As to what women's distinct nature consisted in, Cobbe thought this largely remained to be seen (Cobbe 1862: 605), because women were only now gaining the chance to express it. Still, the art of Bonheur, Browning, and Hosmer made clear that true female difference would have nothing to do with weakness and timidity. In their art, a new female power and physicality was coming into being.

3.3 Cobbe and the Problem of Marriage – Slavery Comparisons

Cobbe may have likened patriarchal marriage to being gobbled up by a tarantula, but the more typical comparison feminists made was with slavery. Comparisons between patriarchal marriage and slavery have a long feminist history, going back before Wollstonecraft and running forward to Beauvoir and after. Cobbe herself said of such comparisons: 'I have always abjured the use of this familiar comparison in speaking generally of English husbands and wives, because as regards the upper orders of society it is ridiculously overstrained and untrue' (Cobbe 1878: 61). But she thought it applied to the working class, and, in any case, she did also say that husbands generally have over their wives 'a power the same as that of a slave-holder of the South over his slave' (Cobbe 1868b: 785) and that:

> To cramp every faculty and cut off all large interests, and then complain that a human being so treated is narrow-minded . . . is . . . an injustice parallel to that of some Southern Americans . . . [who] detail the vices of the negroes which *slavery had produced*, as the reason why they were justified in keeping so degraded a race in such a condition. (Cobbe 1862: 606)[7]

Examples could be multiplied, but evidently Cobbe did *not* always abjure the slavery comparison.[8]

Family/slavery comparisons present a host of problems, as anti-racist and intersectional feminists have argued (see, inter alia, Allen and Allen 1974, Caraway 1991, Ferguson 1992, Gines 2014). At worst, these comparisons trade on the idea that it is terrible for upper-class white women to be reduced to the level of enslaved black people – where in Cobbe's time, of course, slavery remained vital to the American South (the US would formally abolish slavery only in 1865). To be fair, Cobbe actively opposed American slavery. She condemned slave owners as being 'centuries behind the world' and was a founder member of the London Ladies' Emancipation Society in 1863, together with, amongst others, the black abolitionist Sarah Parker Remond. Remond had emigrated from America in 1859, and Cobbe had heard her speak and was influenced by her. Remond held that slavery degraded slave owners and slaves alike, but slave owners the most: 'With all the demoralizing influences by which they are surrounded, they [the slaves] still retain far more of that which is humanizing than their masters' (Remond 1842: 28). Remond argued that, while slaves remain under these demoralizing influences, 'it is really unjust to apply to them the same test, or to expect them to attain the same standard of excellence, as if a fair opportunity had been given to develop their faculties' – which surely influenced Cobbe's almost identical formulation of the same argument, which I quoted just above. Putting all this together, Cobbe thought that it was bad for marriage to be like slavery *and* that this was bad because slavery was *itself* bad, for all those it touched.

---

[7] In the nineteenth century, the word 'negro' was in standard use to mean 'black person', employed by black and white authors alike and not meant pejoratively.

[8] For an excellent analysis of Cobbe's slavery comparisons and their links with imperialism, see Hamilton (2001).

However, there is another problem with family/slavery comparisons. Whenever one says that patriarchal marriage is *like* slavery, one presupposes that the women affected by patriarchal marriage are only metaphorically but not literally slaves. After all, the point of the comparison is to connect two situations that are different. Thus, when women's subjection is traced to the patriarchal family and this is compared to enslavement, the women so subjected are presumed not to be literal slaves but to be in a different condition, comparable to, but not actually the same as, slavery. It is thereby assumed that normally a woman is neither a slave nor an ex-slave, and hence that 'woman' means '*white* woman' unless otherwise specified.

We see Cobbe treating white women as the norm in this way in various places, including *The Duties of Women* when she differentiates the *subjection* suffered by modern European women from the *abjection* undergone by women in the global South and East (Cobbe 1881a: 21–22). For Cobbe, European women are recognised to be rational moral agents, because modern Europe is at a relatively advanced level of civilisation. European civilisation thus violates its own principles in subjecting women and not allowing them to exercise their agency in social practice. This injustice drags Europe down below its proper level. By implication, there is little prospect of non-European women obtaining equal treatment until their societies first reach a higher civilisational level – for in the 'lands of Eastern sensuality, ... woman is first of all the slave of her own weakness, and *then inevitably* the slave of man' (Cobbe 1863: 55; my emphasis). These views led Cobbe broadly to support the British empire on the grounds that it raised less advanced cultures up the civilisational ladder (she also supported British rule in Ireland, seeing the Celts as a backward race). All of which means that Cobbe *did* in part assume that the subjection of white European women was bad because they were being treated in ways that fell beneath their proper standing as white Europeans.

Cobbe thus had some unappealing Victorian-establishment views about European superiority and the civilising mission, and these views form a strand in her position on women. Nonetheless, much else in her writing on women remains inspiring and exciting – and with a welcome streak of humour. Cobbe was a major historical advocate and theorist of women's rights, and she deserves to be recognised as such.

4 The Claims of Animals

4.1 Cobbe's Turn to Animal Welfare

In 1863, Cobbe turned to what, even more than women's rights, would become the driving political passion of her life: animal welfare. The occasion was press coverage of the routine use of vivisection without anaesthetics at the Veterinary College in Alfort near Paris, France.

> The operations [on horses] lasted eight hours, and the aspect of the mangled creatures, hoofless, eyeless, burned, gashed, eviscerated, skinned, mutilated in every conceivable way, appalled the visitors, who reported the facts, while it afforded, they said, a subject of merriment to the horde of students.
>
> (Cobbe 1894: vol. 2: 246–7)

Vivisection – i.e., dissection of, and by extension experimentation on, living animals – was by then well-established in parts of mainland Europe, including France. Now that it was becoming more standard in British medicine and physiology too, Cobbe was worried. In response, she tells us, 'I endeavoured to work out ... the ethical problem ... of a definition of the limits of human rights over animals. ... It was, so far as I know, the first effort made to deal with the moral questions involved' (247). Her account of these 'limits of human rights over animals', based on the moral theory of *Intuitive Morals*, was set out in 'The Rights of Man and the Claims of Brutes', first published in *Fraser's Magazine* in 1863 and then included in *Studies New and Old of Ethical and Social Subjects* in 1865. Cobbe's account is as follows.

4.2 'The Rights of Man and the Claims of Brutes'

4.2.1 The Duty of Benevolence

First, one of our fundamental duties is to minimise the sufferings and promote the happiness of other sentient beings. This is the duty of benevolence. In terms of scope it applies to all sentient beings, animals as much as humans, because all sentient beings can either suffer or be happy. Cobbe sees no difference in kind between human happiness and animal pleasure, defining happiness simply as 'enjoyment of pleasure and freedom from pain' (Cobbe 1865: 223).

4.2.2 Precedency of Benevolence

Second, however, in practice, we cannot simply show complete benevolence to all and sundry. Nor should we try to; we must accord 'precedence in [our] benevolence ... to certain persons above others ... on certain obvious principles of selection – propinquity of blood, contract of marriage, debts of gratitude, &c' (224). This does not

> abolish the claims of more remote objects of benevolence, but only ... subordinate them; that is, when any degree of equality exists between the wants of the nearer and further claimants, the nearer has ... precedence ...

But when the want of the nearest claimant is altogether trifling, and the want of the remoter claimant urgent and vital, the prior claims of the first cannot be held to supersede those of the second ... (224–5)

4.2.3 Human Precedence

Third, from the above two principles, humans have 'precedency of benevolence' over animals. For, unlike animals, human beings are moral agents, which makes humans superior to animals. As moral agents, humans are capable of virtue as well as happiness, and virtue is a more important and ultimate goal than happiness. Because human agents have a higher purpose in life than happiness, their claims take priority over those of animals as long as both sets of claims are real and significant.

4.2.4 Practical Consequences

Fourth, this means that humans may legitimately deprive animals of happiness or cause them to suffer when this is necessary to satisfy basic human 'wants' or needs (228–9), which include the need to investigate and discover the truth – as in medical research – and to educate others in the truth – as in medical teaching (231–2). But we may not harm animals to satisfy 'trifling' wants or merely 'gratuitous' or 'wanton' desires (229). The purposes for which we are harming animals must be serious, meaningful, and incapable of being fulfilled in any other way. Causing harm must be strictly necessary for the purpose in hand. In this respect, anaesthetics are a game changer (233–4). Now that they are available, we must always use them when conducting animal research, otherwise we are wrongly inflicting suffering that is avoidable. The only exception is when animals' pain responses are under investigation; inflicting felt suffering is then unavoidably necessary (234).

4.3 The Structure of Cobbe's Animal Ethics

Cobbe's position derived from her ethical theory in *Intuitive Morals*. She argued there that we must follow the moral law for its own sake. When we do so, we achieve virtue; virtue thus derives from duty, not the other way around: 'Virtue we must not regard as if it were the end for whose production the Moral Law might be considered as a contrivance' (Cobbe 1855: 9). In turn, virtue has priority over happiness (Cobbe 1855: vii), because our primary goal in life is to be virtuous and happiness is secondary. After all, only if we have first learnt to be motivated by duty (i.e., to be virtuous) can we rightly order our own and others' respective claims and so perform the duty of benevolence at all.

More specifically, Cobbe held in *Intuitive Morals* that the moral law requires us (1) to pursue our own virtue – our first priority is to follow the law and cultivate the dispositions that enable us to do so, this being the precondition of our performing any other duties. (2) Next in the order of priority, we must assist other rational agents to attain virtue. (3) Only then does the duty come in to 'love our neighbours' by showing them benevolence. This comes after the duty to assist others towards virtue, because, for all rational agents, virtue takes priority over happiness (Cobbe 1865: 223). In the case of animals, though, duty (2) does not arise, and we only owe them benevolence. By the same token, assisting other rational agents towards virtue takes priority over treating animals benevolently, so that, overall, we must give humans 'precedency of benevolence' because human happiness is a conduit to humans achieving their higher purposes, which does not arise regarding animal happiness (226).

In 'Rights of Man', Cobbe was expanding on what the moral law substantially requires of us. Furthermore, she was charting a middle course between Kantian and utilitarian approaches to animals. Her first premise, that the duty of benevolence pertains to animals because they can suffer or be happy, recalls Bentham's famous statement that 'the question is not, Can they *reason*? nor, Can they *talk*? but, Can they *suffer*?' (Bentham [1789] 1970: 283). However, Cobbe appeals to Joseph Butler in support of her duty of benevolence, and sees Bentham merely as making a welcome return to Butler's principle:

> The world owes to Bishop Butler the exposition of that ultimate ground of moral obligation on whose broad basis stand our duties to all living beings, rational and irrational. He says that if any creature be sentient – i.e., capable of suffering pain or enjoying pleasure – it is cause sufficient why we should refrain from inflicting pain, and should bestow on it pleasure when we may. That is enough. (Cobbe 1865: 222; and see Butler [1726] 2017: 55).

Cobbe appeals to Butler rather than Bentham, because, as we have seen, she believes that utilitarianism cannot adequately account for duty. Kant comes closer to doing so with the idea that we are rational moral agents, responsible for obeying the moral law. But because Kant distinguishes humans, as rational moral agents, from animals, which are merely sentient beings, he ranks humans far above animals in status, and so maintains that humans have no direct duties to animals, only indirect ones. That is, for Kant, we should be kind to animals only because this fosters the dispositions of kindness which we owe to other human agents. Conversely, 'he who is cruel to animals becomes hard also in his dealings with men' (Kant [1784–5] 1997: 212). Cobbe calls this theory of indirect duties 'an enormous error':

> Such a doctrine ... would introduce the same hateful system of morals towards the brutes as that which has too often polluted human charity, – causing it to be performed, not for the benefit of the receiver, but the moral and spiritual interest of the giver. ... We are bound to consider the welfare of the brutes for their sakes, not ours, and because they are so constituted as to suffer and enjoy. That is the moral principle of the case.
>
> (Cobbe 1865: 241)

Cobbe modifies Kantianism, then, to say (with Kant) that the concept of duty entails that humans are rational agents, which raises us above animals in status, but (against Kant) that this leaves room for direct duties to animals. For one of our fundamental duties as rational agents is to foster the happiness of all sentient beings, and although genuine and serious human wants take priority over the needs of animals, this still leaves space for animal needs to trump merely trivial, wanton, and unimportant desires on the part of human beings.

4.4 Cobbe's Later Self-Criticisms

Cobbe's conclusions may sound uncontroversial, or as she said, 'surely almost self-evident' (Cobbe 1865: 230). Even so, clearly no principles remotely like hers were being followed at Alfort, and she feared that British medicine was about to head down the French route unless self-evident principles were given a firm and reasoned statement.

Cobbe later became highly critical of 'Rights of Man'. 'In the 30 years ... since I wrote it I have seen reason to raise considerably the "claims" which I then urged on behalf of the brutes', she remarked (Cobbe 1894: vol. 2: 247–8; see also 60). First, she came to find the entire project of rationally deriving duties to animals misguided. Animal ethics needs to start from feelings. Someone who avoids harming animals merely because rational principles enjoin it may still feel cold and hard of heart towards animals. But it is, above all, the lack of sympathy and affection for animals that leads humans to mistreat them, and this emotional situation is what needs, above all, to change.

Second, 'Rights of Man' provided philosophical grounds for restricting and regulating vivisection but not for abolishing it. According to 'Rights of Man', vivisection was legitimate if it used anaesthetics and was done for the serious purpose of discovering and disseminating the truth. This, too, Cobbe came to think quite misguided, becoming convinced that vivisection was wrong absolutely. To get to her later reasons for opposing vivisection altogether, we must first work through the intermediate steps in her intellectual development, beginning next with her philosophy of mind.

5 Philosophy of Mind

5.1 Harmonising Science and Religion

In the 1860s, Cobbe sought to harmonise science and religion. In 'Rights of Man' she proclaimed:

> 'Science' is a great and sacred word. When we are called on to consider its 'interests' we are considering the cause of that Truth which is one of the three great portals whereby man may enter the temple of God [i.e., the True, the Good, and the Beautiful]. Physical science, ... is in its highest sense a holy thing. ... The love of Truth for its own sake ... has here one of its noblest fields
>
> (Cobbe 1865: 231).

At that time, physiologists were demonstrating that our brains perform many of the cognitive and practical functions previously attributed to the immaterial soul. These demonstrations seemed to leave the soul with little work to do, which diminished the grounds for believing in souls at all, with threatening implications for religion. As part of her programme harmonising science and religion, Cobbe intervened to argue that one could fully embrace physiological knowledge about the brain, body, and nervous system and yet still uphold the immortality of the soul. 'It is my very ambitious hope to show, in the following pages', she explained in 'Unconscious Cerebration', published in *Macmillan's Magazine* in 1870,[9]

> that should physiology establish ... that the brain performs all the functions which we have been wont to attribute to 'Mind', that great discovery will stand alone, and will not determine, as supposed, the further steps of the argument; namely, that our conscious selves are nothing more than the sum of the action of our brains during life, and that there is no room to hope that they may survive their dissolution. (Cobbe 1870b: 24)

5.2 'Unconscious Cerebration'

Cobbe states at the start of her essay that she is combatting the materialist view that thought, consciousness, and the self entirely depend on the brain. That view entails that the self cannot possibly survive the brain's death, so that personal immortality is impossible. She describes this view as follows:

> 'The brain itself', according to this doctrine, 'the white and grey matter, such as we see and touch it, irrespective of any imaginary entity beside, performs the functions of Thought and Memory. To go beyond this all-sufficient brain, and assume that our conscious selves are distinct from it, and somewhat else beside the sum-total of its action, is to indulge an hypothesis unsupported by

---

[9] It is one of Cobbe's several essays on the mind: Cobbe (1866) (1871), (1872b), (1874b: 1–120), and (1875).

a tittle of scientific evidence. Needless to add, the still further assumption, that the conscious self may possibly survive the dissolution of the brain, is absolutely unwarrantable'. (24)

In response, Cobbe accepts that *thought* depends on the brain – she endorses the statement '"Thought is a Function of Matter"' (25). But she distinguishes the *thinking brain* from the *conscious self*: 'the conscious self is not identifiable with that Matter which performs the function of Thought' (25). Because the conscious self and the thinking brain are distinct, it is at least possible that the former can survive the death of the latter.

To back up this distinction of conscious self from thinking brain, Cobbe argues that the vast majority of our practical and intellectual processing is done unconsciously. To see how this provides a backing for her distinction, we must examine what she says about unconscious thought. The brain, she argues, carries out our mental processing according to its own mechanisms and mostly automatically – i.e., where we are either unaware of this processing, or have no control over it, or both. She marshals a large number of examples – of dreams; habitual behaviours like walking and playing the piano; and 'psy' phenomena such as hearing voices, seeing ghostly apparitions, and performing actions while hypnotised or asleep. She spends considerable time documenting how 'unconscious brain-work', operating on laws 'still half unexplained', produces all the rich phenomena of dreams as well as many artistic creations and imaginings (27).

Cobbe did not come up with this idea of unconscious thought out of nowhere. As she noted, William Hamilton had talked of 'latent thought' (Hamilton 1859) and British physiologists had identified the physical basis of these operations in the brain and nervous system. Cobbe especially drew from William Benjamin Carpenter, the most influential physiologist in nineteenth-century Britain, whose *Principles of Human Physiology* was the standard textbook for the teaching of medicine.

In the fifth edition of the *Principles*, Carpenter theorised 'unconscious cerebration'. He distinguished the cognitive and 'ideo-motor' operations performed automatically by the brain from those operations over which we exercise conscious control. He rejected the 'materialism' of Harriet Martineau and her interlocutor Henry George Atkinson in their *Letters on the Laws of Man's Nature and Development* (Martineau and Atkinson 1851), according to which:

> all the operations of the Mind are but expressions or manifestations of material changes in the brain; ... thus Man is but a thinking machine, ... his fancied power of self-direction being altogether a delusion.
>
> (Carpenter 1855: 771)[10]

---

[10] Martineau and Atkinson's book (1851) was a byword for materialism and hugely controversial; for one of the many criticisms, see Froude (1851).

In contrast, Carpenter insisted that '*conscious volitional* agency ... is the essential attribute of Personality' (786). On the one side, we have the brain, body, and nervous system; on the other side we have consciousness, which is constantly correlated with the centre of sensory impressions – the 'sensorium' – but is not identical with it. For Carpenter, the sensorium is rather like Descartes' pineal gland: it is the point where soul and body interact and where there occurs 'the metamorphosis of mind-force into nerve-force and *vice versa*' (543), which enables voluntary action in one direction and in the other enables (some) sensory impressions to reach consciousness. Not all cerebral or ideo-motor operations are voluntary; many of them occur automatically without the soul becoming involved and without ever reaching consciousness. But these non-conscious cerebral operations, Carpenter maintained, do *not* count either as unconscious reasoning (589) or unconscious thought (Carpenter 1871: 211). Both are contradictions in terms, because reasoning and thought are necessarily conscious, requiring the co-operation of the immaterial soul. So, he spoke instead of 'unconscious cerebration', meaning 'operations performed automatically by the cerebrum'.[11]

Although Cobbe takes up the phrase 'unconscious cerebration', she argues that what Carpenter branded as mere 'cerebration' *is* thought after all.[12] From her examples of unconscious processes, she infers that the brain can unconsciously remember, understand, imagine, perform habitual activities, count time, and reason. On the latter, Cobbe is firm that the brain can unconsciously reason, as when it works out the solution to a problem one had consciously put aside (Cobbe 1870b: 29). Therefore, the brain can unconsciously think, because 'it would be an unusual definition of the word "Thought" which would debar us from applying it to the above phenomena, or compel us to say that we can remember, fancy, and understand without "thinking" of the things remembered, fancied, or understood' (35).

---

[11] The word 'cerebration' went back to William Engledue. In his contentious opening address to the London Phrenological Association in 1842, he embraced 'Materialism', defined as the view 'that organised matter is all that is requisite to produce the multitudinous manifestations of human and brute cerebration' (Engledue 1843: 7). Thus, Carpenter was relocating *cerebration* from a materialist register to a dualist one. As Alison Winter (1997) shows, Carpenter carefully separated himself from the materialists in order to establish his respectability.

[12] Cobbe and Carpenter were friends and had many exchanges. For instance, in late 1873, he sought her feedback on his draft book *Principles of Mental Physiology*: 'I shall very much like to know what you think of them' (i.e., of his drafts); 'I feel so very much the value of [your criticisms] that I shall carefully reconsider every point you have suggested' (Cobbe 1855–1904, Carpenter to Cobbe, Sept 4 1873, CB 91; Cobbe, 1855–1904, *Correspondence*, Huntington Library, San Marino, CA.). Published the following year, the book refers to Cobbe extensively (Carpenter [1874] 1875: 372, 457m 519–20, 584–90). Cobbe was shortly to part company with him, as she did with many erstwhile interlocutors, over vivisection.

Given how extensively the brain operates without consciousness, Cobbe then argues, it follows that when consciousness *is* present – i.e., when we are conscious of what we are thinking or doing – this is evidence that 'there is another agency in the field' – another agency 'besides that automatically working brain', because the latter is not as such the organ of consciousness (37). By the same reasoning, on the occasions when we exert conscious control over our mental or practical processes, this other non-cerebral agency is again the one doing the controlling. This agency is the 'Conscious Self' (37) – which, as the agency of control, is also the seat of responsibility, including moral responsibility. Furthermore, because the conscious self is a different agency from the thinking brain, the former may be able to persist independently of the brain after the latter dies. Cobbe thus finishes her essay by quoting Ecclesiastes 12:7: 'when the dust returns to the dust whence it was taken, the Spirit – the Conscious Self of Man – shall return to God who gave it' (37), interpolating the middle clause about the conscious self.

Cobbe took it, then, that we can learn from science about how the brain performs our cognitive functions while retaining Christian faith in personal immortality. She was a dualist, but a singular one, and not a Cartesian dualist: for Descartes, all thought is necessarily conscious, whereas for Cobbe much thinking is *un*conscious. And she went a long way towards physiology, even further than Carpenter, for he did not go so far as to attribute *thought* to the automatically working brain, but Cobbe did; and because she treated the *mind* as the sum total of functions of thought, she also treated the mind as a function of the brain. For these reasons, Cobbe was regularly misunderstood to be a materialist and criticised for it: e.g., by Anonymous (1873) and 'E. V. N.' (1870). Yet, as she was at pains to point out to these critics, she was not a materialist, because she denied that the (brain-based) mind was identical with either the soul, the self, or consciousness.

5.3 Hutton's Criticism

In the 1860s, Richard Holt Hutton co-edited the broadly Anglican and progressive *Spectator*, a journal that reviewed and favourably discussed many of Cobbe's books and essays. For instance, its 1865 review of Cobbe's *Studies New and Old of Ethical and Social Subjects* eulogised her as the female Mill, saying that Cobbe stood as far above other women as Mill did above other men (Anonymous 1865b). As for her 'very interesting and thoughtful essay' on the mind, Hutton appreciated it but made two criticisms (Hutton 1870: 1314):[13]

---

[13] The *Spectator* had a policy of anonymity, but Hutton's pieces are identified in Tener (1973).

(1) Every conscious perception, e.g., of a piece of paper, is made up of innumerable small impressions so minute individually that we cannot possibly be conscious of them all separately. In Cobbe's terms these micro-impressions occur unconsciously and so belong to 'brain-work'. But these countless infinitesimally small impressions add up to conscious perceptions. Therefore the conscious perceptions must also be the result of 'brain-work'. Cobbe has proved too much: it follows from her argument that consciousness is an effect of the brain, even if not all brain-work reaches the level of consciousness (Hutton 1870: 1315).

(2) In any case, actually there can be no unconscious thought – 'thought without will is … a contradiction in terms' (1315). Much of what Cobbe takes to be automatic is really done with conscious will, though we do not remember it because we are so used to exercising will and attention that we immediately and continuously forget having done so.

Having made similar criticisms of Cobbe's 1871 follow-up essay on 'Dreams as Instances of Unconscious Cerebration', Hutton concludes that her 'arguments … are quite insufficient to establish the very important conclusion which Miss Cobbe draws from them [i.e. that mind and thought are functions of the brain], unless they are sufficient to establish very much larger conclusions instead' – i.e., that the conscious self is a function of the brain too (Hutton 1871: 409). Cobbe's position either leads ineluctably into full-blown materialism or, to preserve dualism, she must give up attributing thought to the brain.

5.4 Cobbe's Change of Mind

Perhaps due to these criticisms, and perhaps because she kept being misunderstood as a materialist, Cobbe subsequently changed tack. She abandoned the unusual dualism of 'Unconscious Cerebration' in favour of a more straightforward, traditional dualist stance.

A further factor prompting this change was her reflection on what life in the afterlife might be like. This was in the two-part essay 'The Life After Death' (Cobbe 1874b: 1–120). For Cobbe, our souls must make moral progress in the afterlife – otherwise there is little point in believing in the afterlife at all. 'The *end of creation* I believe to be *the perfecting of souls*' (Cobbe 1881a: 32). But to continue perfecting themselves in the afterlife, our souls must retain moral responsibility for their actions in life. This presents two problems. First, it seems to require that our souls can remember having done these actions. But this appears to be impossible if the soul is disembodied while memory depends on the brain. Second, to retain moral agency and keep making moral progress, the soul must continue to intuit the moral law. For Cobbe, 'intuit' includes 'grasp using reason', as when we deduce what follows from the pure concept of duty. The soul in the afterlife must, therefore, be able to deduce, reason, and think. Yet, if thinking depends on the brain, then the disembodied soul cannot do these things either.

Cobbe considers whether the soul acquires a new spiritual body with some organ that sustains memory and reasoning as the brain does for us now. But she finds it easier to conceive of the soul thinking without a body than to conceive of a new kind of body that would do everything that the brain now does without itself being material (Cobbe 1874b: 74–6). It follows, though, that thought cannot be entirely dependent on the brain after all. If the soul can reason, remember, make moral choices, reflect on its actions, etc., without a brain, then the dualists were right all along: the soul merely uses the body and brain as its organ.

In the end, then, Cobbe's attempted harmonisation of personal immortality and cerebral physiology did not hold. Her religious and moral commitments won out over the scientific ones. This pattern, we will see, would recur and intensify.

6 Criticisms of Evolutionary Ethics

6.1 Cobbe, Darwin, Evolution, and *The Descent of Man*

In the 1860s, when Cobbe was endeavouring to harmonise science and religion, she accepted Darwin's account of the evolution of life and of the species by natural selection in *The Origin of Species* (Darwin 1859). Like many Victorian intellectuals at the time, Cobbe took it that God created nature and life and established the laws regulating the evolutionary process. That process was a progressive, upward ascent, eventually producing human bodies with suitably developed physical and mental powers into which God could infuse our souls and with which we could realise our divinely intended vocation as rational and moral agents. She therefore said:

> That the doctrine of the descent of man from the lower animals, of which Mr. Darwin has been the great teacher, should be looked on as well nigh impious by men not mentally chained to the Hebrew cosmogony, has always appeared to me surprising. ... But that, beyond ... prejudices, there should lurk in any free mind a dislike to Darwinism on religious grounds, is wholly beyond comprehension. (Cobbe 1872a: 2)

Darwin himself seemed to agree that evolution and Christianity were consistent at the conclusion of *Origin* (Darwin 1859: 490), though his actual views were in flux, and he would eventually declare himself an agnostic.[14]

In the late 1860s, Cobbe and Darwin became friends. He was then finishing *The Descent of Man*, the follow-up to *Origin*; specifically, he was writing the parts of *Descent* which dealt with human beings and their moral feelings and

---

[14] Darwin to John Fordyce, 7 May 1879, DCP-LETT-12041 (Darwin Correspondence Project 2008).

practices (Richards 1989: 189–90). Here, Darwin was combatting two other views. One combined evolution and Christianity along the same lines as Cobbe – on which evolution applied to humans only as physical beings, while they also had souls and moral faculties created directly by God. Darwin instead insisted that human beings were entirely natural and evolved in all their properties and powers, the mental and moral ones no less than the physical. However, he also disagreed with those who drew the moral that 'selfish competition' was written into nature. Chief among these was Greg, Cobbe's earlier antagonist on the 'surplus women' issue. Greg (1868) suggested that natural selection mandated the survival of the strongest, most aggressive, and competitive individuals, but that modern society – with its merciful punishments, respect for freedom of thought, and institutions of care and charity for the weak – was making a worrying departure from nature. Against Greg, Darwin argued in *Descent* that, because humans are group animals, selection pressures over time have fostered our instincts to sympathise with others, seek social approval, and adjust our behaviour to co-operate with the group. Natural selection favours *not* selfish competition but social co-operation. But by the same token, we need not invoke divine creation to account for altruism and social conscience: we can get these out of nature.

Cobbe and Darwin discussed ethics at this time, and Cobbe was one of the three people (the others being Alfred Russel Wallace and Saint George Jackson Mivart) whom Darwin singled out to receive advance copies of *Descent* for review (*Descent* appeared in February 1871).[15] However, Cobbe's 'review' – the long essay 'Darwinism in Morals', published in the *Theological Review* in April 1871 – was a stinging critique of Darwin on morality.

6.2 Cobbe's Objections to Darwin

Since Cobbe's objections were many, I shall highlight those that are most illuminating about her own philosophical stance and its development.

6.2.1 Contingent Morality

Contrary to Darwin, treating morality as the outgrowth of natural processes puts it on an insecure basis. For, had the evolutionary pressures on and circumstances of collective human life been different, we would have formed very different moral responses and come to perceive completely different things as being obligatory (Cobbe 1872a: 10–11). Only if moral imperatives are legislated by

---

[15] On Cobbe and Darwin's correspondence over ethics, *Descent*, and related matters, see Stone (2022a). Cobbe herself gives a lively account of their exchanges and how they deteriorated (Cobbe 1894: vol. 2: 123–9).

God do we have a basis for morality that stands independent of circumstances, so that (for example) murder is always and absolutely wrong, not wrong only when we happen to feel so or when circumstances incline us against committing it. To be sure, for Darwin, things could not possibly have been any different, because human beings are intrinsically social animals, which ensures selection for socially co-operative traits. But for Cobbe, what we need is not for murder to be wrong for beings circumstanced and evolved as we are but for it to be wrong absolutely. Thus, for Cobbe, Darwin has made moral requirements contingent in the sense of being dependent on circumstances. What is needed, though, is not for the circumstances to be mercifully fixed, but for basic moral requirements not to depend on circumstances at all.

6.2.2 Cruel and Selfish Instincts

It is important that morality not depend on our nature because plausibly, contrary to Darwin, evolutionary pressures have after all given us dispositions to act selfishly, compete, and trample the weak underfoot. Cobbe refers here to Greg (Cobbe 1872a: 18) – not to endorse his pro-competition conclusion, but to agree with him that the struggle for scarce natural resources has exerted a selection pressure in favour of brutal competitiveness and aggression. Unlike Greg, though, Cobbe thinks this is why it is right and good that modern societies are departing from principles of natural selection; this is a moral advance. Even if Darwin is right that some social traits have been bred into us, she concedes, these are not the *only* traits that evolution has favoured. But then we cannot rely on our inherited traits to secure morality. It requires an independent, transcendent source – in God.

6.2.3 Ahistoricism

Reinforcing her second point, Cobbe contends that Darwin's account is ahistorical (20–3). He projects back onto primitive proto-humans the cultivated, sociable feelings of the Victorian gentleman, and fails to reckon with the true savagery of primitive hominids – which, moreover, lives on in the savagery of both 'primitive' people and supposedly more civilised modern people, as we see in 'wife-torture' and cruelty to animals.

6.2.4 The Utilitarian Dimension

Cobbe's criticisms of utilitarianism come into play, for she locates Darwin within the utilitarian tradition (Cobbe 1872a: 5–8).[16] As she sees it, Darwin addresses an internal tension in utilitarianism. It began as the 'private

---

[16] So did Darwin himself (Darwin 1871: vol. 1: 98).

eudaimonist' view that everyone, in fact, wants and should be free to pursue their own happiness, but Benthamite utilitarians reintroduced a duty to increase the general happiness. However, Cobbe says, according to utilitarianism, people generally have no motivation to obey this duty because they are purely self-interested. Darwin plugs this gap by explaining how our evolved nature instinctually disposes us to feel concern for others and for the common good (6–10). Nonetheless, the ultimate problems of the parent theory persist. Quite simply, for Cobbe, it is not always right to do what promotes the general welfare (15). For example, she says, some tribes practice euthanasia for the good, indeed the survival, of the tribe, but they still recognise that what they are doing is wrong, although, regrettably, it is unavoidably necessary. Thus, our ideas of right and utility are distinct, and the ideas are distinct because right and utility really are distinct, and we intuitively apprehend as much (17).

6.2.5 The Cultivated Bee

Cobbe's objections come together in her discussion of Darwin's hypothetical example of the 'cultivated bee': if bees were conscious and rational, then cultivated worker bees would in times of need see it as their 'sacred duty' to murder their brothers, the unproductive drones. '[T]he bee, or any other social animal, would in our supposed case gain, as it appears to me, some feeling of right and wrong, or a conscience' (28, quoting Darwin). Here, Cobbe says it is Darwin's suggestion that if the circumstances of human collective life had been different, more like that of bees, then we would have evolved so as to regard quite different classes of action as right, such as murder – which, in fact, is absolutely wrong (31). The 'cultivated bee' example confirms the insecure basis on which Darwin has set morality (30). Moreover, since the bees are doing what is useful for the whole hive, the example confirms once more that doing what serves the general good is not necessarily right and may be wholly wrong.

Cobbe concluded: 'The bearings of [Darwin's] doctrine on Morality and on Religion seem to be equally fatal. The all-embracing Law has disappeared' (31). This did not mean that we should reject evolution as applied to life, animal species, and humans as physical beings. What must be rejected was only Darwin's stance that humans are completely evolved in all respects including their moral feelings and judgements. Cobbe rejected not evolution but evolutionary *ethics*, or 'evolutionism', the extension of evolution to account for all of human life and action. She rejected it, more than anything else, because she thought it mandated cruelty to those who are weaker – women, animals, the old, the infirm – whether because they must be sacrificed for the good and health of the whole species or group, or because the strongest must be allowed to push themselves forward, or both (Cobbe 1889: 65–7).[17] Darwinism, in her view, was supremely dangerous because it yielded 'a code of Right in which every cruelty and every injustice may form a part' (Cobbe 1871: 31).

6.3 Critics: Sidgwick, Darwin, Buckley

Darwin was dismayed by Cobbe's critique. In correspondence, he assured her that the bee case confirmed that he *had* made morality secure, because the bees were acting for the common good.[18] Henry Sidgwick came to his defence. Against Cobbe, Sidgwick argued that Darwin's claim was the innocuous one that in different circumstances, different courses of action would advance the general happiness. Darwin's view did not entail that basic moral *principles* could have been or could ever possibly be different, for even the bees were acting for the good of the whole hive, following the principle that we must increase the general welfare. Darwin had thus securely established that we are naturally motivated to follow this basic moral principle (Sidgwick 1872: 231).

Darwin concurred and added a footnote, siding with Sidgwick against Cobbe, to *Descent* (Darwin 1874: vol. 1: 99). Cobbe was unconvinced, because her anti-utilitarian worry remained unanswered. If cultivated bees can commit murder in the service of the general welfare, then clearly serving the general welfare is not necessarily right, and right and utility cannot be the same thing.

A more satisfactory response to Cobbe's worry came from the philosophical science writer Arabella Buckley. At first, in 1871, Buckley defended Darwin, agreeing that he had firmly grounded pure unselfish morality in our evolved nature. Concerning the bees, Buckley said, they are still acting from duty to the community, although what their community needs differs from what a human community needs. Thus 'an action may become a sacred duty to the community in the case of the hive-bee which we know from fact not to be the law of our being' (Buckley 1871: 51).

But Buckley was obviously not satisfied, for she took up the issue again in her 'evolutionary epic' *Life and her Children* (Buckley 1881).[19] The book traces the evolutionary progression of the invertebrates up to their highest level, the ants. But ants, like bees, still

---

[17] Thus, in *Hopes of the Human Race*, she again argued that if 'our personal intuitions of Duty are the inherited prejudices of our ancestors in favour of the ... actions which have proved on experience to be most conducive to the welfare of the community, ... [then] how does it happen that we have all ... a very clear Intuition that it is our duty to preserve the lives of the aged, of sufferers by disease, and of deformed children? ... Yet what, in truth, is this ever-growing sense of the infinite sacredness of human life but a sentiment tending directly to counteract the interest of the community at large?' (Cobbe 1874b: lxxiv)

[18] Emma Darwin to Cobbe, 14 Apr 1871, DCP-LETT-7684F (Darwin Correspondence Project 2008).

[19] On Buckley's 'evolutionary epics', see Larson (2017).

do not have any feeling of sympathy for each other. ... [They] care for the members of their own nest, but more as parts of the community than as individuals. ... [T]he great guiding principle in ant-life appears to be devotion to the *community*, much more than to *each other*.

(Buckley 1881: 298–99; my emphasis)

'Love and personal devotion' only develop in the vertebrates, Buckley explains. By implication, worker bees will kill drones for the sake of the whole, because bees serve the common good but lack sympathy for one another *as individuals*. The vertebrates, however, do develop parental and filial feelings of sympathy for one another as individuals, feelings that then extend into concern for the common good. For vertebrates, sympathy with other individuals is at the root of the co-operative instinct. Therefore, *contra* Cobbe, we need not fear a situation like that of the murderous hive-bees. Our consciences, if we listen to them, will prevent us from sacrificing our siblings and fellow beings for the sake of the whole.[20]

6.4 Cobbe's Subsequent Trajectory

By the time Buckley made these points, it was too late to cut any ice with Cobbe, whose criticisms of Darwin marked a turning point in her thought, doing much to convince her that religion and science could not be harmonised. Her harmonisation programme thus broke down on several counts:

(1) In philosophy of mind, as we saw in section five, Cobbe concluded by 1874 that 'mental automatism' and personal immortality were irreconcilable.

(2) Regarding evolutionary ethics, she concluded that Darwinism justified cruelty in the name of following nature. Darwin thought otherwise; but, for Cobbe, he was mistaking the implications of his own theory.

(3) To Cobbe, the fact that evolutionary ethics was actually a code of cruelty was confirmed when Darwin and his friend and supporter Huxley became two chief opponents of the proposed bill to regulate vivisection on which Cobbe worked in 1875 (see section ten). This drove the final nail into the coffin of the Cobbe–Darwin friendship; from then on, they were enemies, personally and theoretically.

---

[20] Buckley does not mention Cobbe by name, but she would have known Cobbe's essay, for from 1864–75 Buckley was secretary to the distinguished geologist Charles Lyell, a close friend and interlocutor of both Cobbe and Darwin. Buckley, Cobbe, Darwin, and Lyell all moved in the same circles, and from the mid-1860s onwards Cobbe and Lyell saw one another most weekends (Cobbe 1894: vol. 2: 84). In July 1873 Lyell wrote to Cobbe that he had been reading her articles in the *Theological Review*, in which 'Darwinism in Morals' appeared (Lyell 1881: 451–3); this letter was transcribed by Buckley, who handled much of Lyell's correspondence, further showing that Buckley knew Cobbe's views.

7 Heteropathy and Sympathy

7.1 Cobbe's Turn to the Emotions

From her engagement with evolutionary ethics and with Darwin's view that morality rests on our sympathetic and social impulses, Cobbe came to think that the emotions were more important for ethics than she had previously realised. The emotions, she now held, are 'the most largely effective springs of human conduct' (Cobbe 1888b: 223). To obey the moral law, we need to feel emotionally disposed to do so. In particular, to be motivated to treat others benevolently as the law requires, we need to feel sympathy for them, sympathy being defined as pleasure in the other's pleasure and pain at their pain (Cobbe 1874b: 152). Benevolence is thus sympathy realised in action – specifically action to enhance the other's pleasure and reduce their pain (Cobbe 1874b: 154).

However, we cannot rely on our evolved nature to make us sympathise with others. By nature, we have many cruel, vicious instincts. Sympathy comes from elsewhere: we have to be cultivated and educated in it, above all through religion, and especially Christianity. Cobbe, therefore, proposed that there has been a vast historical process in which our natural cruelty has been progressively overcome by sympathy, in stages tied to the succession of world civilisations and their religious outlooks. She gave her account of this process in 'Heteropathy, Aversion, Sympathy' in the *Theological Review* in 1874, re-included in *Hopes of the Human Race* later that same year (under the new title 'The Evolution of the Social Sentiment'). She said:

> It is the aim of the present paper to urge certain reasons ... for treating the Emotion of Sympathy as a sentiment having a Natural History and being normally progressive through various and very diverse phases; differing in all men ... according to the stage of genuine civilization which they ... have attained. (Cobbe 1874b: 153)

She was not abandoning her belief in the transcendent obligating force of the moral law:

> Nothing in the progress of the *emotion* explains either the existence or the progress of the moral sense of *obligation* ... These cultivated instincts ... are not the Moral sense *itself*, but only that which the Moral Sense *works upon*.
> (Cobbe 1874b: lxxiii)

Nonetheless, it is only by having emotions of sympathy for others that we will be motivated to carry out our obligations towards them, and having these emotions depends on the long historical process which Cobbe theorised as follows.

7.2 Cobbe's Theory of History

At the dawn of history, Cobbe claims, *heteropathy* was the prevailing emotion: pleasure in the other's pain and pain at their pleasure. '[T]he earliest reflected emotion is not sympathetic Pain with Pain, ... but ... Displeasure towards Pleasure' (Cobbe 1874b: 176). To provide evidence of heteropathy, Cobbe appeals to direct observations of children and animals, and to ethnographic observations of 'primitive' tribes (notably Tylor 1871). All these are revealing about earlier, less cultivated periods in human history. Animals will often attack and destroy the sick, wounded, aged, or weak: 'at the sight of Pain animals generally feel an impulse to Destroy rather than to Help' (Cobbe 1874b: 158). Animals take action to *worsen* the other's suffering – i.e., they show cruelty, the opposite of benevolence – because the animal takes pleasure in the other's suffering. Such practices as euthanasia and infanticide in tribal societies preserve 'the evidence of the early sway of the same passion of Heteropathy in the human race in its lowest stage of development' (159). To be sure, heteropathy is also at work in modern adults – for example, in cruelty to injured animals and helpless children, and domestic violence, as when a husband beating his wife is only roused by her injuries and distress to attack her the more furiously.[21] Such behaviours show that heteropathy remains instinctive in us and is only ever overcome through cultivating agencies such as religion.

Cobbe traces the stages by which heteropathy has given way. Initially, (1) the only sympathetic feelings are those of mothers for their children. Then (2) slave owners or masters start to take selfish pleasure in the happiness of their slaves and subordinates, because they find that happier subordinates serve them better. (3) A degree of sympathy inevitably begins to arise out of conflicts and wars between tribes. Although tribespeople take pleasure in the sufferings of members of enemy tribes, the tribespeople take this pleasure *together*, so they are sympathising with each other's pleasures (in the sufferings of enemies). In these ways, heteropathy inexorably undermines itself.

Through these three forces, heteropathy becomes weakened until it becomes *aversion*, an emotion intermediate between heteropathy and sympathy. Now, instead of jumping in to harm the weak, injured, sick, and infirm, people turn away from and avoid them. This was the level reached by the ancient Greeks and Romans: they were predominantly aversive, managed a little sympathy, and were still given to a good deal of heteropathy, as manifested by institutions like

---

[21] Thus, Cobbe went on to apply the concept of heteropathy in her critique of domestic violence (Cobbe 1878).

the Roman games.[22] Again, though, even these institutions continued to weaken heteropathy, because the audiences were taking sympathetic pleasure in one another's enjoyment of organised displays of cruelty.

The next step was for people to start to feel pain at others' pain. All the 'great religions' have encouraged this feeling (197) – Christianity most of all, as it encourages us to suffer along with Christ on the cross. However, all these religions emerged within societies that had previously been tribal, and so where people were used to feeling sympathy only for their own groups. These limitations crept into the religions, causing them to enjoin sympathy only for those of the same nation, race, caste, or creed. The various world religions thus instil only partial sympathy.

The final step is taken by Christianity, which, in principle, is the religion of universal sympathy. The Christian God is the God of selfless love, of *agape*; for Cobbe, benevolence (i.e., practical sympathy) 'is the best translation ... of the Pauline *agape*' (Cobbe 1881a: 89), the injunction to love one's neighbour as oneself. Insofar as God is our model, then, we are to practice perfect and complete sympathy. Consequently, Christian Europeans increasingly regard any 'barrier to perfect sympathy' as 'a blot on our civilization' (Cobbe 1874b: 199). This civilisation is dissolving all group restrictions on the scope of sympathy: restrictions of geography, race, class, and – finally – species. Sympathy is being extended from 'the Tribe to the Nation, to the Human Race, to the whole sentient Creation' (199–200).

Cobbe admits that this complete extension of sympathy has been a centuries-long process, and that Christianity has often fallen short of its own standards, particularly in its attitude to animals. But it is now time to realise the Christian spirit of *agape*, for instance, by abolishing slavery everywhere and ending racial inequalities, thereby taking 'the enormous stride' over 'this barrier of race' (191); by instituting 'organised Charity' in such forms as hospitals and social welfare provision (187); and, of course, by outlawing cruelty to animals (207). She concludes:

> Such is, I believe, the great Hope of the human race. It does not lie in the 'Progress of the Intellect', or in the conquest of ... nature; not in the ... more harmonious adjustment of the relations of classes and states; ... But that which will truly constitute the blessedness of man will be the gradual dying

---

[22] Hutton, although sympathetic to Cobbe's account ('so much in this book ... is true and able'; Hutton 1875: 114), objected that she had missed the degree of sympathetic pain with pain already present in the ancient Greeks (114). He also objected to 'the rather oppressive word "heteropathy" ... It seems to us that "antipathy", – which by no means expresses "hatred", as she would have us think, would convey her meaning much better'.

out of his tiger passions, his cruelty and his selfishness, and the growth within
him of the godlike faculty of love and self-sacrifice. (218)

On Cobbe's account, then, history has progressed first through a change in
the *character* of our predominant emotions, with heteropathy being sup-
planted by aversion and then sympathy; and, second, through a change in the
scope of sympathy which is successively extended over more and more
barriers. These two axes of progression mark out four main stages of
civilisation: primitive tribal societies, dominated by heteropathy; classical
civilisations, dominated by aversion; societies based on the non-Christian
religions, governed by partial sympathy; and Christian societies, governed
by complete sympathy.

Cobbe's essay displays an intriguing mixture of optimism and pessimism.
On the optimistic side, she sees sympathy dissolving all barriers and the whole
of history tending necessarily in this direction. On this side, she sometimes
suggests that the old heteropathy is being literally bred out of human beings,
on the grounds that we can inherit acquired traits (169–70).[23] On the pessimistic side, she thinks that heteropathy is alive and kicking, and cannot be
culturally eliminated, because acquired traits *cannot* be passed on biologic-
ally. Here, she was influenced by Francis Galton's work on heredity. In 1870,
she had enthusiastically discussed his *Hereditary Genius*, in which he argued
that nearly all human traits are innate and unchangeable (Galton 1869; Cobbe
1870a).[24] This was the perspective to which Cobbe leaned more, and so she
saw sympathy as a fragile cultural achievement, maintained only under the
influence of religion and other civilising agencies like law, but where each
generation arrives in the world with heteropathic instincts and has to be
civilised again from scratch.

Another pessimistic element was that Cobbe discerned forces at work undermining the civilising agencies of law and religion. Unrestrained vivisection was giving
scientists' heteropathic urges a new outlet, and evolutionism was vindicating people
in acting on their cruel urges, both in vivisection and wider society. For Cobbe,
modern Europeans were at grave risk of falling back below the level of civilisation
they had reached. She went on to warn Europeans in the direst terms: 'Either the
moral progress of Europe must be arrested and recede far back behind the point
attained at the Christian era, or Vivisection must cease' (Cobbe 1889: 271).

---

[23] She was influenced here by Carpenter (1873).
[24] Galton was, of course, also the central theorist of eugenics, which Cobbe rejected: 'our
compassion for the feeble and the sickly ... Mr. Galton considers ... to involve nothing short
of a menace to the civilization whence it has sprung. Nature kills off such superfluous lives
amongst the brutes', and for Galton so should we (Cobbe 1874b: lxxv). For Cobbe, conversely, if
nature is cruel and brutal, all the more reason *not* to follow nature.

7.3 The Shortcomings of Sympathy

Cobbe was chiming in with a huge chorus of talk about sympathy in late nineteenth-century Britain. In different ways, for example, both Dickens and Eliot thought that the central purpose of literature was to arouse our sympathy for ordinary people, leading their everyday lives and taken up with mundane concerns. Critics feared that the rise of sympathy was producing an excessively sentimental and feminised culture. The *Saturday Review*, the conservative rival to the *Spectator*, took this line. The anonymous author of the 1876 essay 'The Shortcomings of Sympathy' argued that:

(1) In practice sympathy is always partial. We do not sympathise with everyone all the time; we sympathise with the particular individuals to whom we are well-disposed, for just so long as we feel well-disposed towards them – so that sympathy is fickle and fluctuating (Anonymous 1876: 315).

(2) Our sympathies for others are rightly limited by other moral judgements and considerations, for instance, whether we believe that someone deserves sympathy or has brought their misfortune on themselves (316).

(3) We therefore cannot realistically expect to see a universal extension of sympathy cutting across all lines including that of species:

> How far it is possible by the highest conceivable kind of self-culture to overcome these obstacles and to attain to a power of sympathizing ... with every kind of human and even brute [i.e. animal] misery ... we cannot attempt to decide here. ... It *seems* highly desirable to cultivate the power of realizing and participating in every kind of suffering ... On the other hand, it is by no means desirable to be ready to pity alike all kinds of sufferers ...
>
> (316; my emphasis).

Universal sympathy is neither practical nor desirable.

Cobbe is not mentioned by name in this piece, but, plausibly, she is one of those targeted: the passage just quoted seems clearly to speak to her ethical vision, her animal welfare activism was making her a byword for sentimentalism, and the *Saturday* featured many critical discussions of Cobbe.[25] Earlier, for

---

[25] Identifying *Saturday* authorship is difficult because the journal had an exceptionally strong corporate voice (Craig and Antonia 2015). Bevington [1941] (1966) matches many articles to authors, but only from 1855–68 and, unfortunately, without covering any Cobbe-related material. However, the 'Shortcomings of Sympathy' author was likely James Fitzjames Stephen, a prolific *Saturday* contributor, for he had made almost identical criticisms (again anonymously) of 'sentimentalism' and unbridled sympathy in *Cornhill Magazine* (Stephen 1864a; my thanks to Carolyn Burdett for the pointer). If so, this reinforces the suspicion that he was in part targeting Cobbe, for he had explicitly criticised her before, again anonymously (in Stephen 1864b: esp. 244).

instance, its review of her *Ethical and Social Subjects*, which included 'Rights of Man', had complained that she made unnecessarily heavy weather of animal welfare. She presented a complex philosophical framework when simple common sense sufficed to tell us that gratuitous animal experiments without anaesthetics were wrong (Anonymous 1865a: 702). Later the *Saturday* objected to Cobbe's denunciation of 'Wife-Torture in England': she had 'palpably exaggerated' the extent of male cruelty (Anonymous 1878: 431). The reviewer was unpersuaded by *heteropathy*: 'a name invented by Miss Cobbe, which seems to denote cruelty of disposition' (431).[26] Thus, whenever Cobbe recommended change – whether through legal reform or expanded sympathies – the *Saturday* bridled. Conversely, when Cobbe took the more conservative side on any question, as when she debated religion with Vernon Lee, the *Saturday* was more approving (Anonymous 1883).[27]

These political factors aside, the *Saturday*'s objections to Cobbe's vision of universal sympathy were not unreasonable: that sympathy is intrinsically bounded by our particular relationships with others and our further moral judgements and principles, so that universal sympathy is neither possible nor desirable; and that sympathy has a place in our moral lives, but it cannot and should not do everything.

Cobbe herself, it may be worth noting, sought to turn the sympathy of her readers away from vivisectors and violent husbands. She had argued that heteropathy inexorably turns into sympathy when people sympathise with others who are enjoying cruel pleasures. But, reciprocally, sympathy has a way of turning back inexorably into heteropathy. For, if we sympathise with those who are suffering, then we will tend to feel antagonistic to those who are causing them to undergo these sufferings. Cobbe would have seen it as quite right that our heteropathy towards these individuals should be aroused.[28] But, in

---

[26] The *Saturday*'s policy was deliberately to solicit unsympathetic reviews. Cobbe later (Cobbe 1902) criticised them for thus indulging the very heteropathy they declined to recognise. Shortly after the critical review of her *Ethical and Social Subjects* came out, the editor, John Douglas Cook, invited Cobbe to join its roster. She replied: 'Tell Mr. Cook that if his review of my "Studies" was a fair and just one I am not good enough to be his contributor. If it was unfair and unjust, his Review is not good enough for me' (Cobbe 1902: 658).

[27] Alexis Antonia used a computational statistics methodology (developed by John Burrows) for tracing *Saturday Review* authorship (Antonia 2009). She has greatly helped me by applying it to some of the journal's pieces on Cobbe, which suggests that Leslie Stephen, James Stephen's brother, may have authored Anonymous (1865a) and (Anonymous 1883). Leslie Stephen regularly contributed to the *Saturday* from 1865–75 but may have contributed occasional later pieces too, especially (Anonymous 1883) given his special interest in agnosticism. He and Cobbe were friends (Cobbe 1894: vol. 2: 16, 57, 59, 116, 244, 261). Antonia's methods suggest that the author who criticised Cobbe on the subject of 'wife-torture' was, however, someone different. I am very grateful to Antonia for her help.

[28] Some heteropathy surely finds an outlet in Cobbe's amusing dramatic parable 'Science in Excelsis' (Cobbe 1877b), in which the angels explain to humanity's scientific representatives why they are going to be vivisecting human beings.

that case, sympathy is not our only ethical source; heteropathy has a place in our moral lives too.

8 Against Atheism

Having come to see Christianity as a fragile bulwark against heteropathic cruelty, Cobbe witnessed with unease the rise of the interlinked currents of atheism, agnosticism, secularism, and freethought. The National Secular Society was founded in 1866, Huxley coined the word 'agnosticism' in 1869, and in the 1870s prominent figures like Annie Besant openly avowed atheism and extolled its moral merits. The last straw was the posthumous publication of Harriet Martineau's *Autobiography* in 1877.

8.1 Martineau's *Autobiography*

In her *Autobiography*, Martineau narrated how she gradually abandoned the Unitarian faith in which she had started out.[29] This was not a classic Victorian crisis of faith of the type that the young Cobbe and Besant had undergone. For Martineau, relinquishing Christianity did not occasion distress and soul searching but afforded overwhelming relief and happiness. At long last, she said, she had

> got out of the prison of my own self, wherein I had formerly sat trying to interpret life and the world, – much as a captive might undertake to paint the aspect of Nature from the gleams and shadows and faint colours reflected on his dungeon walls. I had learned that, to form any true notion whatever of . . . the affairs of the universe, we must take our stand in the external world.
> (Martineau 1877: vol. 2: 333–4)

As she put it elsewhere, 'the relief is like that of coming out of a cave full of painted shadows under the free sky, with the earth open around us to the horizon' (Martineau and Atkinson 1851: 219). The religious life was tormented, selfish, narrowly self-preoccupied, full of 'anxious solicitude about my own salvation' (221). Liberated from these religious illusions, Martineau said, she was now 'with the last link of my chain snapped, a free rover on the broad, bright breezy common of the universe' (Martineau 1877: vol. 1: 89) – out of the cave and in sunlit reality.

Martineau simultaneously relinquished her belief in immortality:

> I feel no reluctance whatever to pass into nothingness, leaving my place in the universe to be filled by another. The very conception of *self* and *other* is, in

---

[29] Unitarianism, so called because its proponents held that Jesus was not literally divine but only an exceptionally good man, was a very influential if heterodox school of Christianity in nineteenth-century Britain. Those it influenced included Darwin, Carpenter, Mill, Hutton, and Cobbe herself.

truth, merely human, and when the self ceases to be, the distinction expires.

(Martineau 1877: vol. 2: 207)

Martineau's happiness at dispensing with God and immortality alarmed Cobbe. Moreover, Martineau was adamant that one could have a purer, less selfish morality without these beliefs. Being liberated from a narrow preoccupation with one's personal virtue and salvation enabled one to contemplate and act in the world in a genuinely disinterested way. This challenged Cobbe's view that God, duty, and immortality were inextricable.

8.2 'Magnanimous Atheism'

To defend her position, Cobbe wrote 'Magnanimous Atheism', which came out in the *Theological Review* in 1877 and was included in her 1882 collection *The Peak in Darien*.[30] She contended that atheism was not a 'magnanimous' creed, as Martineau believed, but a 'burden and a curse' (Cobbe 1882b: 5). The reasons were as follows.

8.2.1 The Afterlife

Martineau was happy that her death would end her personal existence and the world would carry on without her. Cobbe objects that generally we cannot be happy about this (Cobbe 1882b: 46–8). First, death threatens to separate us forever from those we love (this, she holds, is the central respect in which death is bad). Second, we need to believe in an afterlife to reconcile us to our moral failings and those of others, and generally to the imperfections of the world around us. Only a religious framework, in which our souls will continue to perfect themselves in the afterlife, can make our imperfections and failures tolerable and give us hope. Without this, we cannot possibly feel happy at the prospect of our deaths. Martineau deprives us of the Christian framework that we need in order to maintain any happiness in the face of death (66–7).

8.2.2 Selfishness and the Afterlife

Martineau claimed that Christianity enjoins people to act virtuously only for the sake of rewards in the afterlife, reducing virtue to selfishness. For example, Martineau – who was a very passionate abolitionist – unfavourably compared William Wilberforce's motivations for anti-slavery to those of Thomas Clarkson:

---

[30] It is the first of Cobbe's trilogy of anti-atheist essays of this period, together with Cobbe (1883) and (1884).

> Some one was one day praising Wilberforce ... for his toils and sacrifices on behalf of the slave. 'Oh! You know I must,' said the good man ... 'You know I must do this work, for the sake of my salvation. I must save my immortal soul'.... At another time ... a pious friend admonished Clarkson ... whether he had not been neglecting the safety of his immortal soul ... 'My soul! ... I have been so busy about those poor negroes, that I don't think I have thought at all about my own soul'. (Martineau and Atkinson 1851: 247)

Cobbe protests that this is a misrepresentation, because the posthumous reward for a virtuous life is not happiness in a material or affective sense, since after death we will no longer be embodied. Rather, the posthumous reward for virtue is more virtue. This will only make us happy if we value virtue for its own sake. Thus, anyone who acts morally merely for selfish benefits in the afterlife is taking the very attitude that puts posthumous happiness out of their reach (24–5).

8.2.3 How Are Virtuous Agnostics Possible?

Cobbe acknowledges that Martineau was praiseworthy and highly virtuous, like George Eliot. (Cobbe associates the two women, because they had undergone comparable intellectual journeys. They both lost their faith over the 1840s and subsequently became keen on positivism; moreover, in the early 1850s, the two were close friends and moved in similar radical liberal circles.[31]) But the virtue of Martineau and Eliot does not show that virtue is possible without religion. Rather, it shows that these two women were already steeped in Christian virtue, Martineau by her Unitarian upbringing and Eliot by her evangelical phase as an adolescent.

Cobbe's point goes beyond mere biographical detail. These two women, and countless other virtuous agnostics,[32] have been shaped by an overarching Christian horizon embedded in our art and literature, everyday customs and rituals, legal and political institutions, and social life.

> There is an enormous share of human ideas and feelings not directly or consciously turned towards God, yet nevertheless coloured by the belief that such a Being exists ... In Christendom every idea and every feeling have imperceptibly been built up on the theory that there is a God. We see everything *with Him for a background*. (Cobbe 1882b: 49)

Cobbe asks her readers to stop and reflect on all that we would lose if Christianity were really abandoned. But, one might reply, we would not lose

---

[31] See Postlethwaite (1984).

[32] Cobbe treats agnosticism and atheism as continuous, because, at the time, they generally met each other halfway. They combined into the view that, because all knowledge derives from the senses, God is unknowable (agnosticism), but, therefore, we have no grounds for believing that He exists at all (atheism). For a representative statement, see Besant (1893: 139).

much. Here she says: 'Dr. James Martineau once made in a sermon the startling remark that, "if it could be known that God was dead, the news would cause but little excitement in the streets of Berlin or Paris"' (48). However, she says, despite the indifference of these urban sophisticates, really, the 'news' is of devastating import. It is interesting to note that Cobbe spoke of this 'news that God is dead' in 1877, five years before Nietzsche would talk about it in *The Gay Science* (Cobbe 1882b). Although she attributes the above 'startling remark' to James Martineau (Harriet's estranged brother),[33] he had actually said: 'If tomorrow Atheism were somehow to prove true, ... London and Paris would not feel it as they would the death of a Statesman or a President' (Martineau 1876: vol. 2: 220–1). Clearly, Cobbe's own remark is quite different, and she is the one who refers to the 'news' that 'God is dead'.

In any case, Cobbe continues, if Christianity really were abandoned over the long term, morality would die out with it. Indeed, because our culture is deeply and pervasively based on Christianity, this entire culture – our whole horizon of meaning – would also be demolished if atheism took hold. An abyss of meaninglessness would open up before us (Cobbe 1882b: 70–1).

8.2.4 *Moral Law* versus *Rules of Thumb*

Virtuous agnostics are people for whom moral–religious duty is already second nature. But duty can only become second nature when it is held up as an absolute to be done for its own sake. If, instead, we treat moral laws as rules for how to produce the best consequences – as mere 'Rules of Thumb' or 'Ready Reckoners' (Cobbe 1872a: 28; Cobbe 1882b: 58) – then we will always be justified in setting a rule aside if doing so produces better consequences on some occasion. But then we can never acquire virtue, which is the disposition to do our duty just because it is our duty. The praiseworthy dispositions of virtuous agnostics therefore depend on an absolute moral law that can only be absolute if it is divinely legislated (58–60). Again, the presence of virtuous agnostics presupposes Christianity rather than showing that virtue is possible without it.

Cobbe conceded that she had not shown that atheism was false but that the moral consequences of its widespread adoption would be disastrous. Even that prediction might have seemed falsified by virtuous atheists like Martineau and Eliot, but to Cobbe, their existence only testified to Christianity's lingering moral inheritance. People might, nevertheless, judge that atheism must be adopted, whatever the consequences, simply because it is true. In that case,

---

[33] They fell out after James wrote a vituperative review of Martineau and Atkinson's *Letters*; see James Martineau (1851).

Cobbe said, at least adopt it with mournful regret, not with Martineau's exultant joy (Cobbe 1882b: 45–7, 78).

8.3 Vernon Lee's Criticisms

Cobbe's views attracted many criticisms,[34] including those of her younger friend Vernon Lee, who burst onto the British intellectual scene in the 1880s. Lee's central interest was aesthetics, but she also wrote on ethics, secularism, life after death, the problem of evil, anti-vivisection, evolutionary theory, and pessimism. In the 1883 dialogue 'The Responsibilities of Unbelief' Lee argued, against Cobbe, that atheism *does* have to be adopted just because it is true. Religious illusions are comforting, but we must have the courage to confront reality. Cobbe replied with 'Agnostic Morality', also in 1883; both pieces appeared in the *Contemporary Review*. Cobbe objected that, without a religious framework, there were no grounds for valuing or pursuing truth, or regarding honesty and truthfulness as virtues, in the first place.

Lee immediately wrote a rejoinder, but after neither the *Fortnightly* nor *Contemporary Reviews* would publish it, she eventually made it the second dialogue in her 1886 book *Baldwin: Being Dialogues on Views and Aspirations*. Calling it 'The Consolations of Belief', she placed it after 'The Responsibilities of Unbelief', which opened the collection. In 'Consolations', Cobbe is represented by Agatha, while her opponent, Baldwin, represents Lee.[35]

Baldwin puts to Agatha that her faith is a mere delusion onto which she is holding due to motives of fear, hope, and desire (Baldwin 1886: 84). Agatha disagrees: the world really attests to God's existence and His goodness and majesty (88). Not so, says Baldwin; the world is full of suffering: ' ... try and conceive the condition of merely one dying man, or sick child ... and tell me whether ... [they] bear to us an assurance that the God who made them is a God all love' (90). 'Everything in the world is not good', Agatha admits, 'but everything ... is for the best. ... If there were no temptation, no degradation, ... there could be no purity, no aspiration' (90).[36] All will be redeemed and made good in the afterlife (91).

But, Baldwin says, 'everything fresh that we learn respecting the physical basis of mind ... renders it daily more difficult to conceive the survival of the soul when separated from the body of which it seems uncommonly like a function' (92). The belief in an afterlife is mere wishful thinking. Agatha

---

[34] See also, for example, Besant (1885a).

[35] On Lee and Cobbe's friendship, its connection with these dialogues, and their publication history, see the first volume of Lee's letters (Lee 2017). That Agatha represents Cobbe has been noted before (e.g., by Donald 2019: 196–7).

[36] For Cobbe, without religion, 'the life of Aspiration will be lived no more' (Cobbe 1884: 804).

replies that God would not let us form a deluded belief in the afterlife (94). Baldwin objects that Agatha is reasoning in a circle, defending belief in God based on belief in the afterlife, and belief in the afterlife based in belief in God (94–5). The problem of evil, to Baldwin, is unanswerable: 'the very fact of there being evil in the world militate[s] against the notion of the Creator of this evil caring to compensate it' (105).

Agatha protests that is it not Baldwin who is reasoning in a circle in condemning God by moral standards that presuppose God's existence (108)? No, Baldwin answers, because our moral standards presuppose no such thing but are an inherited product of evolution. Contrary to Agatha (and Cobbe), we can fully explain our moral responses, feelings, and judgements on an evolutionary basis, and these feelings can be both evolved and genuinely altruistic, because natural selection has favoured the social instincts (112–13). We can look forward to a continuing evolution in which we progressively improve human lives in this world – whereas, if there is a God, then evil must be stamped indelibly into the universe, and we must resign ourselves to it (117, 123–5). Agatha remains unpersuaded, as Cobbe did. Lee gives them the final word: 'I prefer to believe in the goodness of God' (126).

9 Duties of Women

9.1 Cobbe's *Duties of Women*

Cobbe's major later statement on women is *Duties of Women*, a series of lectures that were published as a book in 1881. Its direction and tone differ from those of her previous writings on women. Cobbe still argues for women's civil and political rights, but now on the grounds that women need these rights in order to do their duty:

> You will judge ... the ground on which, as a matter of duty, I place the demand for women's political emancipation. I think we are bound to seek it, in the first place, as a *means,* a very great means, of *doing good*, fulfilling our Social Duty of contributing to the virtue and happiness of mankind ...
> (Cobbe 1881a: 180)

Cobbe was especially concerned to combat the conservative objections to the women's movement made by Eliza Lynn Linton in her widely read *Saturday Review* essay 'The Girl of the Period' (Lynn Linton 1868). Linton painted a damning picture of the vanity, triviality, narcissism, and immorality of the 'new woman'. Against Linton, Cobbe re-affirmed the integral link between women's rights and morality. 'If women were to become less *dutiful* by being enfranchised ... then I should say: ... "*Nothing* we can ever gain would be worth such a loss"' (Cobbe 1881a: 11). Happily, though, emancipated women 'will be *more* dutiful than they have ever been' (11–12).

Cobbe admitted that there was a worrying rise in selfishness, hardness of heart, and laxity amongst some 'new women' (e.g., Cobbe 1881a: 24, 158). But this was merely a transitory phenomenon, the side effect of the huge change under-way in women's status. Ultimately, giving women more freedom would neces-sarily strengthen their capacity to regulate their conduct by moral principles. To explain why, Cobbe set out a theory of women's duties based on *Intuitive Morals*.

9.2 Personal and Social Duty

First, Cobbe reiterates that the moral law is divinely legislated, and we must obey it for its own sake (Cobbe 1881a: 28–34). From this, it follows that the first duty of women, as of men, is personal duty.

9.2.1 Women's Personal Duties

Personal duty is duty to oneself, specifically to develop the virtues of character that enable one to obey the moral law. These virtues are chastity, temperance, veracity, courage, and conservation of one's freedom (54). These virtues are the same for women as men: 'all virtues must be really alike for all moral agents' (34). This is because what is right is always and forever right, unchanging for everyone and at all times.

Because personal duty takes priority over duties to others (or social duty), women must put self-care before care for others. Women are justified in looking first to their own moral and spiritual welfare, not from selfishness, but because the moral law requires it. For, unless a woman is personally capable of obeying the law, she will never be able to discharge any duties to others adequately. The injunction that women should selflessly put others before themselves is there-fore self-defeating. A woman who does so will merely be buffeted by competing claims with no principled ground for adjudicating amongst them.

9.2.2 Women's Social Duties

Turning to social duties, Cobbe argues that for women, as for men, the duty to 'conduce' to the virtue of others takes priority over the duty to increase others' happiness. She then organises women's duties to promote the virtue and happi-ness of others in order of precedence corresponding to the nature of women's relationships with them:

(1) Blood ties come first, subdivided into parental duties to children, filial duties to parents, then duties of siblings. For Cobbe, natal family ties precede

marital ties; she emphasises that daughters' bonds with their natal families take precedence over any obligations acquired by marriage.

(2) Next come marital ties. Here, Cobbe focuses on arguing that wives do not have a duty to obey their husbands, for, although that obedience might make husbands happy, it does not conduce to the virtue of either wives or husbands. After this come women's duties as joint heads of household, which include duties to treat any household animals kindly and protect them from mistreatment.

(3) Next come duties to society and social groups – i.e., 'associations of equals for purposes of pleasure, mutual hospitality, visits, entertainments, and so forth' (152) – the realm where the household shades into associations like churches, discussion clubs, etc. Women's duties are to speak truthfully in all these settings and show respect and sympathy to their other members.

(4) Then come political duties: duties to the political community and the nation, to take an interest in matters of public concern, and promote the virtue and happiness of the whole community. To perform these duties, women need political rights:

> [W]e must accept and seize every instrument of power, every vote, . . . to enable us to promote virtue and happiness. . . . [It is] a paradoxical person . . . who should earnestly wish that justice and truth and love should prevail, and yet decline . . . the direct and natural means of influencing the affairs of his country in the direction of justice, truth, and love. (179)

9.2.3 The Whole Structure of Duties

Women's duties to others radiate out in circles, from immediate family through civil society to the state. Each domain of duties requires corresponding rights. In the family, women need rights of civil personality and property ownership, or they will never responsibly use the family finances or exercise prudence in housekeeping. In society, women again need rights of civil personality if they are to be respected and treat others respectfully and conscientiously. In the political realm, as we have also seen, to do their duty to the political community, women must have political rights.

9.3 From Politics to Ethics

Much of Cobbe's position in *Duties* is now totally uncontroversial. Even in 1906, Helen Bosanquet was already remarking that the book seemed 'out of date' because so much that Cobbe advocated had been achieved, even though '[t]he change is one which she [Cobbe] herself had a large share in bringing about' (Bosanquet 1906: 398). But, by the same token, we now have enough distance from the immediate political context of *Duties* to notice its philosophically interesting features:

(1) Cobbe grounds her arguments on *Intuitive Morals*, making an explicitly philosophical case for women's emancipation.

(2) She stresses personal virtue so heavily that we might wonder whether she is gravitating towards a virtue- rather than duty-based ethics. She did not think so herself; generally the Victorians did not categorise virtue ethics as a distinct tradition of ethical theory, and Cobbe always regarded virtue as the consequence of duty rather than its motivation or goal. Insofar as she recognised virtue ethics, it was under the category of *euthumism*, which, as we have seen, she rejected. Even so, in *Duties* the virtues threaten to expand beyond the duty-based framework in which Cobbe places them.

(3) Cobbe is also pushing towards a relational ethics, on which we have distinct obligations to others depending on our relationships with them. This brings her close to the ethics of care, on which our principal ethical goal is to maintain the fabric of relationships. However, by prioritising personal over social duty, Cobbe avoids any suggestion that women should sacrifice themselves to the care of others.

In sum, if *Duties* now looks unexciting politically, this is because its central interest lies elsewhere: in ethics.

9.4 Cobbe's Suffragism and Ward's Anti-suffragism

In *Duties*, Cobbe adopted the popular late nineteenth-century view of society as a set of nested spheres radiating from immediate family through society into national government, and she defended women's civil and political rights as enabling women to fulfil their duties in these several spheres. Ironically, all this meant that Cobbe now shared many assumptions with the woman who spearheaded organised anti-suffragism in Britain: Mrs Humphry Ward (or Mary Augusta Ward, although she preferred to be known publicly under her husband's name).

In Ward's anonymous 1889 'Appeal Against Female Suffrage' (Ward 1889) – signed by 103 women, including Cobbe's adversary Linton – Ward argued that women should not have the vote because there are tight connections amongst national government, industrial policy, high finance, military affairs, and imperial rule. All these are outside women's proper sphere, which is the family and the parts of civil society that naturally extend out of it: education, welfare, and local government. Accordingly, women should have rights to education and to participate in teaching, welfare work, and local government, so that they can perform their duties of care and service in these fields. But women can only perform their duties by staying in their proper sphere, otherwise their moral capacities for care and service will be degraded by the violence, competition, and harsh struggle of the 'male' sphere. Contrary to Cobbe, women can do their duty only by staying out of national government and public affairs.

Cobbe disagreed. For her, women have the same personal and social duties and must cultivate the same virtues as men. However, because Cobbe now made duty the basis of women's political claims, she was actually not that far from Ward's opposing view that, to do their duty, women must have more limited rights than men.[37] After all, Cobbe conceded to Linton that *if* giving women political rights were to diminish women's morality, then she would cry "'For Heaven's sake, let us stay where we are!'" (Cobbe 1881a: 11). Cobbe thought the conditional would not ultimately be fulfilled. But Ward thought that it inevitably would: giving women political rights was bound to diminish women's morality, so the moral case was against giving women such rights. Cobbe had tied women's rights so tightly to their duties that she strengthened the ground on which the anti-suffragists made their case.[38]

10 Anti-vivisection and Zoophily

10.1 The Cruelty to Animals Act 1876

Cobbe did not write about our duties to animals as a merely academic exercise. She wanted change, specifically regulation and restriction of vivisection. Having spent more than ten years lobbying, rousing support, and rallying public opinion, Cobbe prepared a draft bill (Henniker's Bill) to regulate vivisection which her allies put before parliament on 4 May 1875. Under the proposals, vivisection was to be practised only at registered premises undergoing regular inspections, always using anaesthetics except under time-limited personal

---

[37] The shared assumptions enabled Ward and Cobbe to become friends despite disagreeing on suffrage. Cobbe admired Ward's best-selling 1888 philosophical novel *Robert Elsmere,* and Ward gushed back: 'My personal admiration for you dear Miss Cobbe, and your wonderful devotion is boundless' (Cobbe 1855–1904, Ward to Cobbe, 24 May 1894, CB 814–5; Cobbe 1855–1904, *Correspondence,* Huntington Library, San Marino, CA.). Ward invited Cobbe to join the council of University Hall, the pioneering adult education college that Ward started in 1890, eventually renamed the Mary Ward Centre (Cobbe 1855–1904, Ward to Cobbe, 1888–94, CB 806–15; Cobbe 1855–1904, *Correspondence,* Huntington Library, San Marino, CA.). It included a play school for children and facilities for disabled children. Moreover, Ward had previously been instrumental in establishing Somerville College for women in Oxford. She was not the dinosaur we might imagine.

[38] The common ground between suffragists and anti-suffragists is analysed by Julia Bush (2007: 9) and – regarding Ward versus the suffragist Millicent Fawcett – by Delap (2002).

licences. In response, the scientific community rallied, led by Darwin, Huxley, and John Burdon Sanderson. They drafted a rival bill (Playfair's Bill), presented on 12 May, requiring only those performing painful experiments to obtain licences under medical approval, with no system of inspection.

A Royal Commission was set up to investigate and resolve the issue. Its final report recommended a form of regulatory apparatus that compromised between the earlier rival bills. The government now moved to legislate, but leaned back towards animal welfare concerns, and so proposed tighter regulations, the prohibition of all experiments on dogs, cats, and horses, and a requirement of anaesthesia as standard. Last-minute scientific and medical lobbying resulted in the legislation being watered back down. The result – the Cruelty to Animals Act of 1876 – introduced a licensing system closer to Playfair's Bill.[39]

To Cobbe, the Act was a bitter disappointment. By allowing vivisectionists to license one another and so avoid prosecution, it protected the perpetrators, not their victims. She bleakly recalled:

> My hopes had been raised so high to be dashed so low as even to make me fear that I had done harm instead of good, and brought fresh danger to the hapless brutes for whose sake, as I realised more and more their agonies, I would have gladly died . . . Justice and Mercy seemed to have gone from the earth. (Cobbe 1894: vol. 2: 280)

Cobbe now began to see her 'Rights of Man', by then a key reference point for anti-vivisectionists, as part of the problem. She had argued there that vivisection was permissible under certain limitations. In hindsight, this only strengthened the vivisectors' case that, as long as they were monitoring each other, business could proceed as usual. Cobbe concluded that vivisection must be completely prohibited. A key essay in which she put the philosophical case for prohibition was 'Zoophily', published in *Cornhill* in 1882.[40]

10.2 'Zoophily'

10.2.1 Moral before Physical Welfare

Cobbe's first argument in 'Zoophily' has the same premises as 'Rights of Man' but draws a different conclusion from them. Animals are not moral agents but merely sentient beings, so the only factors that bear on their well-being are pleasure and the absence of pain. Conversely, humans are not only sentient but also moral agents, so our moral welfare as well as our happiness must be

---

[39] For an excellent account of these political negotiations, see Hamilton (2004a).

[40] The word 'zoophily' at the time meant love of animals and care for their welfare. It had nothing to do with what is now called zoophilia, i.e., sexual desires for animals.

considered when determining what is right. Pain, then, is the 'supreme offence as regards the lower animals, but *not* the supreme offence as regards man' (Cobbe 1882a: 282). For human beings, moral wrongdoing, not pain, is the supreme offence. Therefore:

> [T]rue ethics bid us regards man's *moral* welfare only as of supreme import-
> ance, and anything which can injure *it* (such . . . as the practice, or sanction of
> the practice, of cruelty), as the worst of evils, even if along with it should
> come a mitigation of bodily pain.

In essence, because our spiritual welfare and salvation take priority over our merely physical flourishing, we must not perform wrong actions – such as inflicting pain on animals – *even if* the longer-term effect is to reduce bodily pain for human beings, e.g., by discovering cures for illnesses.

In 'Rights of Man', Cobbe had argued that because humans are moral agents and therefore are ranked above animals, we may harm animals for the sake of moral and physical benefits to human agents. Now, she argues that precisely *because* humans are moral agents, we may not harm animals, even to benefit other humans, because as moral agents we must, above all, avoid doing wrong.

10.2.2 Sympathy for Animals

Cobbe's first argument begs the question: *Is* it wrong to harm animals if doing so confers longer-term benefits upon other humans (and, indeed, other animals, who may also benefit from medical knowledge)? To show that it is, Cobbe invokes her more crucial argument, that our first duty is to adopt the right feeling towards animals:

> We must perchance yet wait to determine what are the right *actions* of man to
> brute; but . . . we need [not] lose much time in deciding what must be the right
> *sentiment*: the general feeling wherewith it is fit we should regard the lower
> animals. If we can but clearly define that sentiment, it will indicate roughly
> the actions which will be consonant therewith. (281)

This was a major change from 'Rights of Man', where Cobbe provided rational grounds for right action towards animals but regarded our feelings towards animals as fluctuating, unreliable, and subject to cultural variation, so that feelings could only ever supplement rational considerations. Now, on the contrary, it is sentiment that provides the guide for right action.

What sentiments ought we to feel?

> The only befitting feeling for human beings to entertain towards brutes is . . .
> the sentiment of Sympathy . . .; of Pity, so far as we know them to suffer; of

Mercy, so far as we can spare their sufferings; of Kindness and Benevolence, so far as it is in our power to make them happy. (286)

This was not at all a return to Kant's view, which Cobbe had previously criticised, that we must treat animals kindly so as to foster our dispositions of kindness to other humans. For Cobbe, it is *animals*, directly, to whom we have a duty to feel kind.

From this duty to feel sympathetic and kind, it follows that we 'must put an absolute stop to Vivisection. ... Either we must cherish animals – and then we must abolish Vivisection, – or we must sanction Vivisection; and ... poison the springs of pity and sympathy in our breasts' (287). In performing a vivisection, one must treat the animal as a mere mechanism, dealing 'with a living, conscious, sensitive, and intelligent creature as if it were dead and senseless matter' (288). This remains the case even if anaesthetics are used. In experimenting on an animal, even when anaesthetised, we have to stifle and put down our impulsive responses of sympathy and compassion for a fellow creature. We steel and harden ourselves. Over time, this becomes habitual, and it creates room for our vicious, cruel dispositions of heteropathy to come to the fore.

On this basis, Cobbe could identify why the 1876 licensing system was defective. Vivisection degrades the practitioner; it inevitably makes them hardened, cruel, and thus motivated to disregard and seek ways around any restrictions and regulations placed on their activities. Vivisectors cannot be trusted to obey such restrictions, because their practice corrupts (Cobbe 1889: 217). The only solution is prohibition.

10.3 Campaigns and Schisms

Cobbe went on to campaign tirelessly for the abolition of vivisection; the language of 'abolition' drew on the moral force of earlier campaigns for the abolition of slavery. The issue led her to break with many former interlocutors – Darwin, Huxley, Galton, and Carpenter, amongst others. By 1878, she had already made abolition the goal of the Victoria Street Society (VSS), which she had founded in late 1875. The VSS had many prominent supporters, such as Tennyson and Ruskin, who publicly resigned his professorship at Oxford in 1885 when a vivisection laboratory was established there. However, the anti-vivisection movement divided between those favouring abolition and others who thought that the only practical and realistic option was to build on the 1876 Act and pursue further regulation. This schism broke out again and again. Cobbe ultimately came to think that the VSS had become too conciliatory with the reform agenda, and so she started a new organisation, the British Union for the Abolition of Vivisection, in 1898. As this shows, she became increasingly intransigent over time.

Meanwhile, the anti-vivisection movement grew and grew. It hybridised with other currents: suffragism, alternative religions, socialism, and anti-vaccinationism. Vivisection became one of the most contentious issues of the time. Indeed, shortly after Cobbe died, the contention reached a new peak with the Brown Dog riots of 1907, which were instigated by medical students protesting against a memorial that had been erected to a terrier 'done to death in the laboratories of University College' (see Lansbury 1985). Vivisection had split late Victorian and Edwardian society down the middle.

10.4 Anna Kingsford's Criticism

Given Cobbe's centrality to anti-vivisectionism, countless criticisms were made of her arguments.[41] One criticism came from the fascinating and unconventional figure Anna Kingsford, who combined vegetarianism, anti-vivisectionism, spiritualism, Theosophy, and Christian mysticism. In 1872, Kingsford briefly edited the weekly *Lady's Own Paper* and called for contributions on vivisection; Cobbe provided a short piece. Amicable correspondence between the two women ensued. But in 1882, Kingsford sought Cobbe's backing to join the Somerville Club, a discussion society for women. Cobbe refused, and an acrimonious exchange followed which brought the friendship to a rapid end. Cobbe's reasons for blocking Kingsford are not entirely clear. She may partly have wanted to see off a potential rival leader of anti-vivisectionism, for Kingsford was a charismatic figure with the advantage of having a medical degree. But the two women also had a philosophical disagreement. This concerned vegetarianism.[42]

For Kingsford, vegetarianism and anti-vivisection were two sides of the same coin. If it was wrong to harm and kill animals for science, then it was wrong to harm and kill them for food. Cobbe thought otherwise. In 'Rights of Man' she rejected 'vegetarian errors' (Cobbe 1865: 244). She stated that 'we may slay

---

[41] See, e.g., the pro-vivisection essays in Hamilton (2004b). Another interesting criticism came from Lee, who argued in 'Of Honour and Evolution', against Cobbe, that evolutionism provided a basis for anti-vivisectionism (Lee 1886: 127–84). Yet another critic was Besant, who gave a utilitarian defence of vivisection (Besant 1882b), although she subsequently changed her mind, for instance, in 'Against Vivisection: Harmlessness is the Highest Religion' (Besant 1903). Cobbe rejected utilitarian defences partly on slippery-slope grounds (Cobbe 1889: 218).

[42] An excellent account of the failed relations between Cobbe and Kingsford is Vyvyan (1969). Kingsford's intellectual co-worker Edward Maitland also narrates the story but portrays Cobbe as a malign and persecutory presence in Kingsford's life (Maitland 1896).

cattle for food, and take the fowls of the air and the fish of the sea to supply our table' (229), because meat eating is an unavoidable physical necessity for humans. In 'Zoophily', she reiterated that we 'need not sacrifice the higher life for the lower', which was what she took vegetarians to be demanding (Cobbe 1882a: 286). And in 'The Lord was not in the Earthquake', she explained that:

> The all-pervading law by which animal life is chiefly sustained by preying on other life is unquestionably repugnant to our feelings ... Nevertheless, the principle of the law may ... be rightly justified ... and admitted to be compatible with the widest beneficence. Death ... is an inevitable condition attached to physical life. An amount of pain among creatures may be further accepted as needful ... (Cobbe 1888a: 74).

For Cobbe, meat eating and vivisection were not analogous: one was necessary, the other was not.

This was a difficult ground to hold. On the one hand, pro-vivisection scientists thought that vivisection and meat eating were analogous because experimenting on animals was genuinely necessary to find cures for diseases and thus preserve human life. On the other hand, Kingsford argued that the two were analogous because neither was necessary. Vivisection was not necessary but useless, because the 'differences of structure, function, and character between men and animals' prevent any straightforward transference of findings from animals to humans (Kingsford 1882: 177). Moreover, far from being useful, vivisection was positively harmful: it degraded the moral character of scientists and thus debased humanity overall, mistakenly sacrificing human spiritual welfare for the sake of mere physical welfare – sacrificing the higher good for the lower one (Kingsford 1883). Analogously, Kingsford argued, 'flesh-eating' was not necessary for human sustenance or human health, because we can subsist perfectly well on a vegetarian diet. And, further, 'flesh-eating' was positively harmful: a vegetarian diet is healthier for us physically, morally, and spiritually (see Kingsford 1912).

There was a degree of realpolitik in Cobbe's anti-vegetarianism. She thought that the anti-vivisection campaign would be most effective concentrating on a single issue, and she sought to keep it safely distanced from the demi-monde of spiritualism, Theosophy, and socialism. Nonetheless, Cobbe's anti-vegetarianism was a real weak point. Practically, it opened her to accusations of hypocrisy for opposing vivisection while eating meat. And philosophically, if Kingsford was right that meat eating was not necessary for life or health, and was positively damaging to our spiritual welfare, then Cobbe's position was inconsistent. The very same grounds on which she condemned vivisection should have led her to oppose meat eating as well.

11 How Cobbe Became Forgotten

Despite her fame and standing in her own time, Cobbe did not become part of the canon of Western philosophy. On the contrary, after she died, she was rapidly forgotten. The same fate has befallen many historical women philosophers, for reasons that feminist and feminist-informed historians of philosophy have examined: the 'Great Man' paradigm, the reluctance of men (and often women) to reference and acknowledge women's work, the fact that women generally lacked male students and disciples to carry on their ideas, and plain old sexist bias. Even so, given the reputation Cobbe once had, it remains surprising that she did not end up with even a minor part in philosophy's remembered drama of its own history. The explanation, I suggest, lies in the damaging interaction between two parallel developments: Cobbe's anti-vivisection crusade and the emergence of philosophy as a specialist profession.

11.1 The Professionalisation of Philosophy

From the 1870s onwards, a sea change took place in British intellectual life. The academic disciplines started to establish and demarcate themselves, forming their specialist journals, societies, and venues. *Mind* was founded in 1876 and the *Proceedings of the Aristotelian Society* in 1888, the first specialist philosophy journals in Britain. The same pattern held right across the disciplines. For example, *Brain: A Journal of Neurology* was founded in 1878; previously, mind, soul, and brain had been a unified field of discussion amongst physiologists, philosophers, theologians, and others, but now the ways were parting. The earlier generalist culture was receding and a new specialist one was taking its place.

As specialist periodicals and forums were set up, being a credible party to philosophical discussions became increasingly dependent on publishing in the right venues, in the ways approved by members of the profession, and on being part of their community. But to establish philosophy's disciplinary credentials and carve out the new identity of the philosophical expert, practitioners had to distinguish their work from the earlier generalist public culture. In this way, the older figure of the all-round critic and committed public intellectual became displaced by a new persona, the professional specialist or expert. The operative contrasts were *specialist* versus *generalist* and *expert* versus *popular* (or *expert* versus *amateur*). Nascent professionals also distinguished their *neutral* and *detached* work from *partisan* and *sectarian* efforts. Finally, they distinguished their *reputable* work from that emanating from *unorthodox* cultures like Theosophy, anti-vivisection, socialism, or feminism.

The first two contrasts are on show in the 1872 review of Cobbe's *Darwinism in Morals* by Sidgwick, which is significant, because he and Thomas Hill Green are the chief claimants to the title of first professional philosopher in Britain (Brown 2014). Sidgwick recognises that Cobbe's arguments are 'ingenious', yet he bills her an 'excellent populariser' – i.e., a representative of the earlier *popular, generalist* culture, not a specialist expert (Sidgwick 1872: 230–1). He further classifies Cobbe's work as 'partisan', lacking the proper level of neutral detachment. At the time, though, Cobbe's reputation was still high enough for her to merit Sidgwick's respectful review. This was to change.

11.2 Cobbe's Anti-vivisection Crusade

As we have seen, after 1876, Cobbe decided that vivisection must be prohibited. So began her long, bitter, and ultimately doomed struggle against the bulk of the scientific and medical establishment, a struggle that took over her life, with anti-vivisectionism eclipsing all her other interests. As Cobbe's biographer Sally Mitchell puts it, she 'squandered her intellectual credibility' with her tireless and uncompromising crusade for abolition (Mitchell 2004: 284). She was pilloried and ridiculed in the press, portrayed as an over-wrought, sentimental woman. Allegedly, the sensible, rational, male, medico-scientific establishment accepted the need for animal experimentation; ill-informed women headed by Cobbe were obstructing progress.

Cobbe hit back with the (uncharacteristically anonymous) essay 'The Medical Profession and Its Morality' (Cobbe 1881b). She argued that doctors were monopolising control of medicine out of base motives of self-interest, greed, cruelty, and self-aggrandisement. This was a direct attack on the gathering forces of professionalisation, since medicine was the paradigmatic profession: under the terms of the 1858 Medical (Registration) Act, only those who were legally qualified could legitimately practise. Cobbe correctly grasped, and opposed, the sea change that was underway to a culture where only qualified specialists could adjudicate on the specific fields of their expertise.

Others defended that change. *The Times* in 1892 reported on a discussion of vivisection at a church congress at which Victor Horsley declared that:

> Those who considered themselves to be fit to judge upon the question might be divided into three classes – (1) those who knew well the sciences of physiology, pathology, practical medicine, and surgery; (2) those who were ignorant of these sciences; (3) those who knew something, but who deliberately falsified the facts. To the first class belonged the whole body of the

honourable members of the medical profession. To the second and third classes belonged the anti-vivisectionists. ... He described Miss Cobbe's book on the subject as one of the rankest impostures that had for many years defaced English literature. ... Miss Cobbe had deliberately and fraudulently misrepresented the actual facts [of many experiments].

(Anonymous 1892: 6)

Cobbe had been intervening about vivisection in terms of the older culture, in which a generalist could address the public based on their all-round intellectual and moral authority. That culture was disappearing, replaced by one in which only 'honourable members of the profession' had epistemic authority, and others were either ignorant or impostors.

Heated debate ensued in *The Times*, but the research assistant who had gathered the information for the book prefaced by Cobbe to which Horsley referred, *The Nine Circles of the Hell of the Innocent* (Rhodes 1892), actually had misrepresented some of the facts. Cobbe had to concede as much, an embarrassing climbdown that did enduring damage to her reputation (Mitchell 2004: 338–40). Through a succession of similar incidents, Cobbe went 'from being a highly respected religious writer and reformer to one who was criticised and ridiculed' (Williamson 2005: 213). Her star fell precipitously. Even people who remained sympathetic to her now took her to stand for one thing alone: anti-vivisection. Her formidable prior philosophical contribution was forgotten by critics and admirers alike.

Cobbe retaliated by attacking scientists and medical practitioners ever more vociferously, both as members of their professions and, in some cases, personally. Her warnings about the dangers of science and vivisection became apocalyptic. She lamented that scientific medicine was sanctioning a new religion of health, 'hygeiolatry', in which the welfare of the body drove out any concern for the soul (Cobbe 1882b: 77–88). She feared that people were increasingly required, not to exercise freedom of judgement and conscience, but to display 'deference to the opinion of a particular class', namely the scientists (Cobbe 1877a: 39–41, 47). Moral, religious, and aesthetic considerations were being dismissed: 'The claims of the aesthetic faculty, and even of the moral sense, to speak in arrest of judgement on matters entirely within their own spheres, are ruled out of court' (Cobbe 1888c: 4). Cobbe had travelled a long way since she declared science sacred in 1865. She now considered science utterly inimical to any sense of the sacred and closer to the demonic.

Yet, it was the rising culture of scientific expertise on whose terms fledgling professional philosophers sought to establish themselves. Their goal was to be reputable, impartial, detached, and rational. Meanwhile, Cobbe had come to epitomise sentimental and partisan concern for animals – as when her opponent

Elie de Cyon, for instance, lambasted anti-vivisectionism in the *Contemporary Review* as 'coarse fanaticism', 'unscrupulous', and driven by 'hysterical old maids' (Cyon 1883: 500). By the time that Cobbe died in 1904, hers was not a name with which any would-be professional philosopher would have wished to be associated.

11.3 Why Have Feminist Philosophers Not Recovered Cobbe?

In 1913, the novelist G. K. Chesterton wanted to show that nineteenth-century women had contributed little to philosophy. He began: 'I never heard that many women, let alone men, shared the views of Mary Wollstonecraft; I never heard that millions of believers flocked to the religion tentatively founded by Miss Frances Power Cobbe' (Chesterton 1913: 91). He rejected Wollstonecraft's and Cobbe's claims to philosophical significance – but they were the two women that he took to have the strongest such claims. Yet, whereas Wollstonecraft has since been recovered by feminist philosophers and restored into the canon of Western philosophy, Cobbe has not. Why?

11.3.1 Being Mainstream

Susan Hamilton suggests that Cobbe has been neglected because she was part of the establishment. She was at the centre, not the margins, of Victorian culture, and was a big name in the 'established periodical press'; she endeavoured 'to locate feminist thought at the centre of mainstream culture, ... introducing its terms to a wider, non-feminist identified audience' (Hamilton 2006: 8, 12). Ironically, Cobbe's very success may have counted against her, and feminist historians have perhaps assumed that Victorian culture was so patriarchal that women must perforce have had to do philosophy in the medium of literature or in other indirect and out-of-the-way forms and styles. We have been like the police detectives in Poe's story 'The Purloined Letter', who fail to spot the stolen letter hanging from the mantlepiece in plain sight, because they are convinced that it must have been concealed somewhere obscure.

11.3.2 Non-fiction

This point follows directly from the preceding one: Cobbe has been disadvantaged because she wrote non-fiction, as Sally Mitchell observes (Mitchell 2004: 3). Mitchell quotes Frances Willard, who was already pointing out in 1897 that Cobbe 'has taken duty, not love, for her theme, and the essay, not the novel, as her literary vehicle'. Ironically, Cobbe has been neglected precisely *because* she almost entirely wrote non-fiction prose,[43] much of it convention-ally philosophical – stating premises and deriving consequences, setting out arguments for conclusions, defining terms, and so forth.

11.3.3 Cobbe's Politics

As Carol Bensick has pointed out, in the movement to recover historical women philosophers, those who were more mainstream or conservative have often lost out, and 'unconventional women philosophers took priority', as well as those who were more radical politically (Bensick 2012: 28). Cobbe, of course, was very radical in her claims for women and animals, in boldly writing as a woman and supporting herself by doing so, in sharing her life with another woman, and in claiming authority in the philosophical domain. Yet, at the same time, she affiliated herself with the Conservative party,[44] supported the empire, and staunchly defended Christianity albeit in unconventional form. And her central concept was not *rights* but *duties*.

11.3.4 Victorian Periodicals Culture

Many contemporary philosophers have only a limited sense of Victorian print and periodical culture: its scale and diversity, its distinctive features like anonymity and serial debate, and the generalist kind of philosophising that these features made possible. This has hindered us from understanding the kind of philosophising that Cobbe did.

11.3.5 Cobbe's Interlocutors

Many of Cobbe's interlocutors have also been lost from view, such as Carpenter, Hutton, Ward, Besant, Remond, Kingsford, Linton, Martineau, and Lee. To restore Cobbe, we need to remember these others too and populate more of the intellectual space that surrounded her.

11.3.6 Cobbe's Wide-Ranging Oeuvre

No single work of Cobbe's is *the* statement of her views. As she remarked herself, 'In reviewing my whole literary and journalistic life, I perceive that I have been

---

[43] There are exceptions, such as Cobbe's science-fiction dystopia 'The Age of Science' (Cobbe 1877a) – although even this takes the form of an imaginary news report from 1977 rather than a conventional 'story' – and the dramatic parable 'Science in Excelsis' (Cobbe 1877b), men-tioned in section seven.

[44] Cobbe's contemporaries also found it an unexpected affiliation: the London newspaper *The Globe* remarked in 1885, 'It will be news to most persons that Miss Cobbe is a Conservative of long standing' (quoted in Mitchell 2004: 314). In fact, at the very end of her life, in 1901–2, Cobbe abandoned the Conservatives – over vivisection, women's rights, and her opposition to the South African War – and joined the Women's Liberal Federation (Atkinson 1904: xii).

from first to last *an Essayist*; almost *pur et simple*' (Cobbe 1894: vol. 2: 76). Most of her books are collections of journal articles; she favoured the short-form essay over the long-form treatise. To employ Isaiah Berlin's distinction between 'foxes' and 'hedgehogs' – 'The fox knows many things, but the hedgehog knows one big thing' (Berlin [1953] 1993: 3) – Cobbe was more of a fox. To be sure, like the hedgehog, she had a coherent and comprehensive standpoint that informed everything she addressed; but she was ultimately more like the fox, in 'seizing upon the essence of a vast variety of experiences and objects' (3). Her resulting body of writing is huge. As Francis Newman remarked: 'If she had dealt with only half her subjects, no one would have suspected that she was able to write on the other half' (Newman 1865: 368) – and that was in 1865 when she still had thirty-five years more writing ahead of her.

Given the extent of Cobbe's written work, which is now widely and freely available through online digital archives and repositories, it is again surprising how rarely any of this work is examined. But perhaps the vastness of Cobbe's oeuvre is part of the problem, because the reader scarcely knows where to begin with it. I hope that this Element has addressed this problem by providing a thread through the labyrinth of Cobbe's oeuvre.

Conclusion

I have argued in this Element that Cobbe's ideas and work are worth recovering. She was a vivacious, powerful, and direct writer, whose tone ranged effortlessly from the genuinely funny to the sublimely serious. She did not shy away from addressing big questions and taking bold positions on them. She had her own overarching philosophical perspective, which uniquely synthesises an anti-naturalist and duty-based ethics with theism, feminism, animal welfarism, and other strands besides.

Cobbe did not philosophise in a vacuum either politically, culturally, or intellectually. She had many interlocutors, male and female, and she was an inspiration to younger women like Besant, Kingsford, and Lee. Her ideas were very widely known in her time, as I have indicated with respect to the abundant discussion of her views in the *Spectator* and the *Saturday Review*. It is later historians of nineteenth-century thought who seem unable to see her in the record even though she is there. I suspect that this is because she does not fit our expectations: she was not marginal or counter-cultural, and she was not writing fiction but doing philosophy in forms and places that were accepted and conventional in her time.

As for the interest of Cobbe's ideas and claims, this surely speaks for itself: whether morality must be understood in terms of a moral law and whether this must presuppose a divine legislator; what the ethical implications of evolution-ary theory are and whether they are acceptable to us; what we lose if we abandon belief in the afterlife; whether and under what conditions experimentation on live animals is morally legitimate; whether there is unconscious thought and, if so, what this implies about self, mind, and brain; whether women will in freely realising themselves become more deeply and genuinely female; how to order and prioritise our obligations to ourselves and to the other people in our lives; what place sympathy has in ethics; and whether there has been historical progress and, if so, what the standard of progress is. Cobbe had many important things to say. I hope that we may be ready to listen to her and put her back where she belongs on the philosophical map.

References

Allen, Robert L. and Pamela P. Allen (1974) *Reluctant Reformers: Racism and Social Reform Movements in the United States.* Washington, DC: Howard University Press.

Anonymous (1865a) Miss Cobbe's Ethical and Social Subjects. *Saturday Review* June 10: 701–2.

Anonymous (1865b) Miss Cobbe's New Volume of Essays. *Spectator* July 1: 725–6.

Anonymous (1873) Unconscious Fallacy of 'Unconscious Cerebration'. *College Courant* March 15: 121–2.

Anonymous (1876) The Shortcomings of Sympathy. *Saturday Review* September 9: 315–16.

Anonymous (1878) Miss Cobbe on Wife-Torture in England. *Saturday Review* April 6: 430–1.

Anonymous (1883) Agnostic Morality. *Saturday Review* June 9: 724–6.

Anonymous (1892) Vivisection. *The Times* October 7: 6.

Antonia, Alexis (2009) Anonymity, Individuality and Commonality in Writing in British Periodicals – 1830 to 1890: A Computational Stylistics Approach. PhD thesis, University of Newcastle, Australia. https://nova.newcastle.edu.au/vital/access/manager/Repository/uon: 6075.

Atkinson, Blanche (1904) *Introduction to Life of Frances Power Cobbe.* Expanded ed. Ed. Blanche Atkinson. London: Swan Sonnenschein.

Bensick, Carol (2012) A New Lost Woman Philosopher: Amalie John Hathaway. *CSW Update.* https://escholarship.org/uc/item/6910n7mm.

Bentham, Jeremy (1970) *Introduction to the Principles of Morals and Legislation*, ed. J. H. Burns and H. L. A. Hart. Oxford: Clarendon.

Berlin, Isaiah (1993) *The Hedgehog and the Fox.* Revised ed. Chicago: Elephant Paperbacks.

Besant, Annie (1882a) *The True Basis of Morality.* London: Freethought Publishing.

Besant, Annie (1882b) *Vivisection.* London: Besant & Bradlaugh.

Besant, Annie (1885a) *A World without God.* London: Freethought Publishing.

Besant, Annie (1885b) *Autobiographical Sketches.* London: Freethought Publishing.

Besant, Annie (1893) *An Autobiography.* London: T. Fisher Unwin.

Besant, Annie (1903) *Against Vivisection.* Benares: Theosophical Publishing.

Bevington, Merle Mowbray (1966) *The Saturday Review 1855–1868*. New York: AMS Press.

Bosanquet, Helen (1906) Review of *The Duties of Women* by Frances Power Cobbe. *International Journal of Ethics* 16(3): 398.

Brown, Stuart (2014) The Professionalization of British Philosophy. In *The Oxford Handbook of British Philosophy in the Nineteenth Century*, ed. W. J. Mander, 619–40. Oxford: Oxford University Press.

Buckley, Arabella ('A.B.') (1871) Darwinism and Religion. *Macmillan's Magazine* 24: 45–51.

Buckley, Arabella (1881) *Life and Her Children*. New York: Appleton.

Bush, Julia (2007) *Women against the Vote: Female Anti-suffragism in Britain*. Oxford: Oxford University Press.

Butler, Joseph (2017) *Fifteen Sermons and Other Writings on Ethics*, ed. D. McNaughton. Oxford: Oxford University Press.

Caraway, Nancie (1991) *Segregated Sisterhood: Racism and the Politics of American Feminism*. Knoxville: University of Tennessee Press.

Carpenter, William Benjamin (1855) *Principles of Human Physiology*. 5th ed. Philadelphia: Blanchard & Lea.

Carpenter, William Benjamin (1871) The Physiology of the Will. *Contemporary Review* 17(April): 192–217.

Carpenter, William Benjamin (1873) On the Hereditary Transmission of Acquired Psychical Habits. *Popular Science Monthly* 3(July): 303–321.

Carpenter, William Benjamin (1875) *Principles of Mental Physiology*. New York: Appleton.

Chesterton, G. K. (1913) *The Victorian Age in Literature*. London: Thornton Butterworth.

Cobbe, Frances Power (anonymous) (1855) *An Essay on Intuitive Morals Volume One: Theory of Morals*. London: Longmans.

Cobbe, Frances Power (1862) What Shall We Do with Our Old Maids? *Fraser's Magazine* 66: 594–610.

Cobbe, Frances Power (1863) *Essays on the Pursuits of Women*. London: Emily Faithfull.

Cobbe, Frances Power (1864) *Broken Lights: An Inquiry into the Present Condition and Future Prospects of Religious Faith*. London: Trübner.

Cobbe, Frances Power (1865) *Studies New and Old of Ethical and Social Subjects*. London: Trübner.

Cobbe, Frances Power (1866) The Fallacies of Memory. *Galaxy* 15: 149–62.

Cobbe, Frances Power (1868a) *Dawning Lights: An Inquiry Concerning the Secular Results of the New Reformation*. London: Whitfield.

Cobbe, Frances Power (1868b) Criminals, Idiots, Women, and Minors. *Fraser's Magazine* 78: 774–94.

Cobbe, Frances Power (1869a) *Why Women Desire the Franchise*. London: National Society for Women's Suffrage.

Cobbe, Frances Power (1869b) The Subjection of Women [review of Mill's *Subjection of Women*]. *Theological Review* 6: 355–75.

Cobbe, Frances Power (1869c) The Final Cause of Woman. In *Woman's Work and Woman's Culture*, ed. Josephine Butler, 1–26. London: Macmillan.

Cobbe, Frances Power (1870a) Hereditary Piety. *Theological Review* 7: 211–34.

Cobbe, Frances Power (1870b) Unconscious Cerebration: A Psychological Study. *Macmillan's Magazine* 23: 24–37.

Cobbe, Frances Power (1871) Dreams as Instances of Unconscious Cerebration. *Macmillan's Magazine* 23: 512–23.

Cobbe, Frances Power (1872a) *Darwinism in Morals, and Other Essays*. London: Williams & Norgate.

Cobbe, Frances Power (1872b) The Consciousness of Dogs. *Quarterly Review* 133: 419–51.

Cobbe, Frances Power (1874a) *Our Policy: An Address to Women Concerning the Suffrage*. London: National Society for Women's Suffrage.

Cobbe, Frances Power (1874b) *The Hopes of the Human Race*. London: Williams & Norgate.

Cobbe, Frances Power (1875) Thoughts about Thinking. *Cornhill* 31: 207–19.

Cobbe, Frances Power (1876) *Re-echoes*. London: Williams & Norgate.

Cobbe, Frances Power (as 'Merlin Nostradamus') (1877a) *The Age of Science*. London: Ward, Lock & Tyler.

Cobbe, Frances Power (1877b) *Science in Excelsis*. London: Victoria Street Society.

Cobbe, Frances Power (1878) Wife-Torture in England. *Contemporary Review* 32: 55–87

Cobbe, Frances Power (1881a) *The Duties of Women*. Boston: Ellis.

Cobbe, Frances Power (anonymous) (1881b) The Medical Profession and its Morality. *Modern Review* April: 296–328.

Cobbe, Frances Power (1882a) Zoophily. *Cornhill* 45: 279–88.

Cobbe, Frances Power (1882b) *The Peak in Darien, with Some Other Inquiries Touching Concerns of the Soul and the Body*. London: Williams & Norgate.

Cobbe, Frances Power (1883) Agnostic Morality. *Contemporary Review* 43: 783–94.

Cobbe, Frances Power (1884) A Faithless World. *Contemporary Review* 46: 795–810.

Cobbe, Frances Power (1888a) The Lord was not in the Earthquake. *Contemporary Review* 53: 70–83.

Cobbe, Frances Power (1888b) The Education of the Emotions. *Fortnightly Review* 43: 223–36.

Cobbe, Frances Power (1888c) *The Scientific Spirit of the Age*. London: Smith & Elder.

Cobbe, Frances Power (1889) *The Modern Rack: Papers on Vivisection*. London: Swan Sonnenschein.

Cobbe, Frances Power (1894) *Life of Frances Power Cobbe*, 2 vols. London: Bentley & Son.

Cobbe, Frances Power (1895) The Ethics of Zoophily. *Contemporary Review* 68: 497–508.

Cobbe, Frances Power (1902) Schadenfreude. *Contemporary Review* 81: 655–66.

Craig, Hugh and Alexis Antonia (2015) Six Authors and the Saturday Review: A Quantitative Approach to Style. *Victorian Periodicals Review* 48: 67–86.

Cyon, Elie de (1883) The Anti-vivisectionist Agitation. *Contemporary Review* 43: 498–510.

Darwin Correspondence Project (2008) *Darwin Correspondence Project*. https://www.darwinproject.ac.uk.

Darwin, Charles (1859) *On the Origin of Species by Means of Natural Selection*. London: Murray.

Darwin, Charles (1871) *The Descent of Man, and Selection in Relation to Sex*. 2 vols. London: Murray.

Darwin, Charles (1874) *The Descent of Man, and Selection in Relation to Sex*. 2nd ed. London: Murray.

David, Deirdre (1987) *Intellectual Women and Victorian Patriarchy*. Basingstoke, UK: Macmillan.

Delap, Lucy (2002) 'Philosophical Vacuity and Political Ineptitude': The Freewoman's Critique of the Suffrage Movement. *Women's History Review* 11(4): 613–30.

Donald, Diana (2019) *Women against Cruelty: Protection of Animals in Nineteenth-Century Britain*. Manchester: Manchester University Press.

Easley, Alexis (2004) *First Person Anonymous: Women Writers and Victorian Print Media, 1830–70*. Farnham: Ashgate.

Engledue, W. C. (1843) *Cerebral Physiology and Materialism*. London: J. Watson.

E.V.N. (1870) Latent Thought. *Spectator* November 12: 1349–50.

Ferguson, Moira (1992) *Subject to Others: British Women Writers and Colonial Slavery, 1670–1834*. London: Routledge.

Froude, James Anthony (anonymous) (1851) Materialism. – Miss Martineau and Mr. Atkinson. *Fraser's Magazine* 43(256): 418–34.

Galton, Francis (1869) *Hereditary Genius*. London: Macmillan.

Gines, Kathryn (2014) Comparative and Competing Frameworks of Oppression. In Simone de Beauvoir's *The Second Sex*. *Graduate Faculty Philosophy Journal* 35 (1–2): 251–73.

Greg, William Rathbone (anonymous) (1862) Why Are Women Redundant? *National Review* 14(28): 434–60.

Greg, William Rathbone (anonymous) (1868) On the Failure of 'Natural Selection' in the Case of Man. *Fraser's Magazine* 78(465): 353–62.

Hamilton, Susan (2001) Making History with Frances Power Cobbe: Victorian Feminism, Domestic Violence, and the Language of Imperialism. *Victorian Studies* 43(3): 437–460.

Hamilton, Susan (2004a) Introduction to *Animal Welfare and Anti-vivisection 1870–1910* Vol. 1: *Frances Power Cobbe*. London: Routledge.

Hamilton, Susan, ed. (2004b) *Animal Welfare and Anti-vivisection 1870–1910* Vol. 3: *Pro-Vivisection Writings*. London: Routledge.

Hamilton, Susan (2006) *Frances Power Cobbe and Victorian Feminism*. London: Palgrave.

Hamilton, Susan (2012) 'Her usual daring style': Feminist New Journalism, Pioneering Women, and Traces of Frances Power Cobbe. In *Women in Journalism at the Fin de Siècle*, ed. F. Elizabeth Gray, 37–52. London: Palgrave.

Hamilton, William (1859) *Lectures on Metaphysics and Logic* Vol. 1. Boston: Gourd & Lincoln.

Hetherington, Naomi and Clare Stainthorp, eds. (2020) *Nineteenth-Century Religion, Literature and Society* Vol. 4: *Disbelief and New Beliefs*. London: Routledge.

Hutton, Richard Holt (anonymous) (1870) Miss Cobbe on Latent Thought. *Spectator* (November 5): 1314–15.

Hutton, Richard Holt (anonymous) (1871) Miss Cobbe on Dreams. *Spectator* (April 8): 409–10.

Hutton, Richard Holt (anonymous) (1875) Miss Cobbe's Hopes for the Human Race. *Spectator* (January 23): 113–15.

Kant, Immanuel (1997) *Lectures on Ethics (1784–5)*, trans. Peter Heath. Cambridge: Cambridge University Press.

Kingsford, Anna (1882) The Uselessness of Vivisection. *The Nineteenth Century* 11(60): 171–83.

Kingsford, Anna (1883) Unscientific Science: A Lecture. Edinburgh: Andrew Elliot.

Kingsford, Anna (1912) *Addresses and Essays on Vegetarianism*, ed. Samuel Hopgood Hart. London: John M. Watkins.

Lansbury, Coral (1985) *The Old Brown Dog: Women, Workers and Vivisection in Edwardian England*. Madison, WI: The University of Wisconsin Press.

Larsen, Jordan (2017) The Evolving Spirit: Morals and Mutualism in Arabella Buckley's Evolutionary Epic. *Notes and Records* 71(4): 385–408.

Lee, Vernon (1886) *Baldwin: Being Dialogues on Views and Aspirations*. Boston: Roberts Brothers.

Lee, Vernon (2017) *Selected Letters of Vernon Lee, 1856–1935,* Vol. I, *1865–1884*, ed. Amanda Gagel. Routledge.

Lyell, Mrs, ed. (1881) *Life, Letters and Journals of Sir Charles Lyell, Bart.* London: J. Murray.

Lynn Linton, Eliza (anonymous) (1868) The Girl of the Period. *Saturday Review* March 14: 339–40.

Maitland, Edward (1896) *Anna Kingsford, Volume 1: Her Life, Letters, Diary and Work*. London: G. Redway.

Martineau, Harriet (1877) *Autobiography*. 3 vols. London: Smith, Elder & Co.

Martineau, Harriet and Henry George Atkinson (1851) *Letters on the Laws of Man's Nature and Development*. London: Chapman.

Martineau, James (anonymous) (1851) Mesmeric Atheism. *Prospective Review* 26(April): 224–62.

Martineau, James (1876) *Hours of Thought on Sacred Things: A Volume of Sermons*. 2 vols. London: Longmans, Green, Reader and Dyer.

O'Connor, Maureen (2017) 'Revolting Scenes of Famine': Frances Power Cobbe and the Great Hunger. In *Women and the Great Hunger*, eds. Christine Kinealy, Jason King, and Ciarán Reilly, 161–72. Cork: Cork University Press.

Mill, John Stuart (1869) *The Subjection of Women*. London: Longmans, Green, Reader and Dyer.

Mitchell, Sally (2004) *Frances Power Cobbe: Victorian Feminist, Journalist, Reformer*. Charlottesville, VA: University of Virginia Press.

Newman, Francis (anonymous) (1865) Capacities of Women. *Westminster Review* 28(2): 353–80.

Nietzsche, Friedrich [1882] (2001) *The Gay Science*, trans. Josefine Nauckhoff. Cambridge: Cambridge University Press.

Peacock, Sandra J. (2002) *The Theological and Ethical Writings of Frances Power Cobbe, 1822–1904*. Lewiston: Edwin Mellen.

Postlethwaite, Diana (1984) *Making It Whole: A Victorian Circle and the Shape of Their World*. Columbus: Ohio State University Press.

Remond, Sarah P. (1842) The Negroes in the United States of America. *Journal of Negro History* 27(2): 216–8.

Réville, Albert (1875) Review of Cobbe, *Hopes of the Human Race. The Academy* 7(167): 56–57.

Rhodes, G. M. (1892) *The Nine Circles of the Hell of the Innocent*, with a preface by Frances Power Cobbe. London: Swan Sonnenschein.

Richards, Robert (1989) *Darwin and the Emergence of Evolutionary Theories of Mind and Behavior*. Chicago: University of Chicago Press.

Sidgwick, Henry (1872) Review of Cobbe, *Darwinism in Morals and Other Essays. The Academy* 3(46): 230–1.

Stephen, James Fitzjames (anonymous) (1864a) Sentimentalism. *Cornhill* 10 (55): 65–75.

Stephen, James Fitzjames (anonymous) (1864b) Life and Writings of Theodore Parker. *Fraser's Magazine* 69(410): 229–45.

Stone, Alison (2022a) Introduction to *Frances Power Cobbe: Essential Writings of a Nineteenth-Century Feminist Philosopher*, ed. Alison Stone. Oxford: Oxford University Press.

Stone, Alison (2022b) Further Reading on Cobbe. In *Frances Power Cobbe: Essential Writings of a Nineteenth-Century Feminist Philosopher*, ed. Alison Stone. Oxford: Oxford University Press.

Taunton, Matthew (2014) Print Culture. British Library, *Discovering Literature*. https://www.bl.uk/romantics-and-victorians/articles/print-culture#.

Tener, Robert H. (1973) R. H. Hutton: Some Attributions. *Victorian Periodicals Newsletter* 6 (2): 1–65.

Tylor, Edward B. (1871) *Primitive Culture*. 2 vols. London: Murray.

Vyvyan, John (1969) *In Pity and in Anger*. London: Michael Joseph.

Ward, Mary A. (1894 24 May) Letter to Frances Power Cobbe. *Frances Power Cobbe Correspondence, 1855–1904*. Box 12, issue/copy CB 814–5, Huntington Library, San Marino CA.

Ward, Mrs Humphry (anonymous) (1889) Appeal against Female Suffrage. *The Nineteenth Century* 25(148): 781–88.

Wellesley Index (2006–21) W.E.H. Wellesley College 29 August 1965 Introduction. http://wellesley.chadwyck.co.uk/marketing/well_intro.jsp.

Williamson, Lori (2005) *Power and Protest: Frances Power Cobbe and Victorian Society*. London: Rivers Oram Press.

Winter, Alison (1997) The Construction of Orthodoxies and Heterodoxies in the Early Victorian Life Sciences. In *Victorian Science in Context*, ed. Bernard Lightman, 24–50. Chicago: University of Chicago Press.

Acknowledgements

I would like to thank all those who have helped me with writing this manuscript: Alexis Antonia and Carolyn Burdett, for help trying to pin down authorship in the *Saturday Review*; Morex Arai at the Huntington Library in San Marino, California, where the Frances Power Cobbe correspondence is held, for help obtaining digital copies of parts of Cobbe's correspondence; the series editor, Jacqueline Broad, for inviting me to write this book and providing enthusiastic support; and the anonymous reviewers, for their very helpful comments.

Women in the History of Philosophy

Jacqueline Broad
Monash University

Jacqueline Broad is Associate Professor of Philosophy at Monash University, Australia. Her area of expertise is early modern philosophy, with a special focus on seventeenth and eighteenth-century women philosophers. She is the author of *Women Philosophers of the Seventeenth Century* (CUP, 2002), *A History of Women's Political Thought in Europe, 1400–1700* (with Karen Green; CUP, 2009), and *The Philosophy of Mary Astell: An Early Modern Theory of Virtue* (OUP, 2015).

Advisory Board

Dirk Baltzly, *University of Tasmania*
Sandrine Bergès, *Bilkent University*
Marguerite Deslauriers, *McGill University*
Karen Green, *University of Melbourne*
Lisa Shapiro, *Simon Fraser University*
Emily Thomas, *Durham University*

About the Series

In this Cambridge Elements series, distinguished authors provide concise and structured introductions to a comprehensive range of prominent and lesser-known figures in the history of women's philosophical endeavour, from ancient times to the present day.

Cambridge Elements ≡

Women in the History of Philosophy

Elements in the Series

Printed in the United States
by Baker & Taylor Publisher Services